How to De-Stress
Your Life

Other books by Gregory Jantz

How to De-Stress Your Life

Gregory L. Jantz

SPIRE

© 1998 by Gregory L. Jantz

Published by Revell
a division of Baker Publishing Group
P.O. Box 6287, Grand Rapids, MI 49516-6287
www.revellbooks.com

Spire edition published 2008

Third printing, January 2009

ISBN 978-0-8007-8769-1

Previously published under the title *Becoming Strong Again*

Printed in the United States of America

Contents

Acknowledgments

I would like to give heartfelt thanks to the co-creator of this book, Robert C. Larson. Bob helped me work through each of the issues presented here—from the earliest note taking through to the completed manuscript. Bob's skills go far beyond writing; he also brings tremendous wisdom and insight into the entire creative process. This book is a remarkable endeavor that could only have been accomplished through the mutual sharing of our hearts. Bob has been my faithful sidekick throughout, and I am deeply grateful.

I also owe a great debt of gratitude to my wife, LaFon, who faithfully stood by me as I struggled through my own period of recovering from emotional exhaustion.

I want to acknowledge all of you who over the years have faithfully encouraged others. Professional counselors and friends with a listening ear, you are the cement that helps hold so much together. Thank you for who you are and for what you do.

To those who struggle with emotional exhaustion and have picked up this book, you have taken a courageous step toward your better future.

I'm also grateful to my colleagues who give generously and passionately from their hearts each day to the vision and work of The Center for Counseling and Health Resources, Inc. You are people who know and live what Bob and I have written of in this book—that we really all *can* find inner healing.

I'd also like to thank the men and women who've given me the privilege of working and journeying with them and who have been so honest and revealing in sharing their struggles. They are the true heroes of this book as they've told their stories of how they are regaining control of their lives. They've shown us again and again that their pain has not been in vain.

Thanks to my editors William J. Petersen and Linda Holland for their passion and belief in this project, the second book to be published with Revell. Without Bill's vision, persistence, and encouragement, this book would not have seen the light of day. Because of his commitment to this project, many people from all walks of life will find the courage to do what it takes to become strong again. Thank you, Bill. Thank you, Linda, for your enormous editing skills. You gave the manuscript your skillful, creative touch. A big thanks to Lois Stück who also put the finishing touch on my previous book *Healing the Scars of Emotional Abuse*. Lois knows how to polish and shine!

Most of all, we thank our Creator for the built-in resilience we all have to become strong again—emotionally, physically, and spiritually.

1

Coming Apart at the Seams

Here is Edward Bear, coming downstairs now, bump, bump, on the back of his head behind Christopher Robin. It is, as far as he knows, the only way of coming downstairs, but sometimes he feels there really is another way, if only he could stop bumping for a moment and think about it.

A. A. Milne
Winnie the Pooh

Dan was a success in every sense of the word. To the average observer this young man had already achieved everything most people think they might want: comfortable home, loving wife, some modest investments that were starting to work—all neatly wrapped in an obsessive, insatiable need to work ten to twelve hours a day in a job where he listened to people spill their guts, share their dreams, confess their iniquities, and plead for his help. Dan was good at providing that help—that was the problem. He was, perhaps, too good, too skilled. So good, in fact, that he felt he was indispensable, a kind of "father confessor" to a growing congregation of the needy. So he kept counseling and counseling, seeing as many as twelve people a day. He had to be there. His people needed him—and so did the state-run halfway house he managed.

Between sessions Dan would eat junk food, make a fast phone call, do some quick paperwork, push himself to the limit, see more people, and fall in bed exhausted at midnight. The next day it was the same routine. His output was incredible. No one could outwork him. Dan was a man with a mission to be the best and the brightest. He didn't know it, but he was also bent on self-destruction.

Instead of honest sweat on a treadmill at the local gym, Dan ran on an unhealthy emotional treadmill that demanded he meet the expectations of others. *Yes, I'd be glad to see you. . . . Of course, I can work you in. No problem, I can skip lunch today and see you at, say, 1:15? . . . What's that? Saturday? I don't think that will be a problem. I was going to be in the office anyway.*

Perhaps it's best to let Dan tell the story in his own words:

"I was strong physically and mentally. I knew I was pushing the envelope with the intensity of my work at the halfway house, but I was confident—stubbornly cocky might be a better way to say it—that I could make a success of it, even though I was counseling people with the same tendencies toward burning the candle at both ends while I looked for creative ways to burn it in the middle also. I lived in full denial that I, too, might have a problem.

"Then, as it happens with so many people, I crossed that invisible line between living a whole, healthy life and what I would probably now call 'temporary insanity.' Not in the clinical sense, perhaps, but certainly a life that was out of control to the point of not knowing who I was, where I was, or what I was doing.

"I started drinking on weekends. Not much at first; just enough to take away the tension. The alcohol numbed my hurts, even as it numbed my spirit. I had crossed the line.

"I had once been regular at church but now had quit. My friends assumed I'd dropped off the face of the earth. If it hadn't been for my wife, who hung in there with me, there's no telling what might have happened. I assigned her as the 'designated worshiper,' while I stayed home and drank. It became obvious to me later that she had her own needs, and her presence in a house of worship eventually became the turning point in her own life and relationship with God.

"I quit exercising—something I'd enjoyed for years. I stopped running, let the bicycles gather dust, put on a paunch, and didn't even care. I quit paying attention to what was important in my life, and I wasn't prepared to accept responsibility for my deteriorating condition. It had to be my circumstances, my work load, unfair people, the government . . . my blame list was endless. The only problem with my list was that my name wasn't on it. Big mistake.

"I became hypervigilant—a time bomb ticking off the minutes until it explodes. I couldn't concentrate, and that's when the depression began to set in. Everything about my life became distorted: I evaluated things as either completely good or totally bad and would either magnify or minimize the significance of an event. Perspective and a sense of balance had gone out the window.

"We no longer invited friends over to visit. Our once active social life went to zero. All the time, I kept drinking—not just on weekends, but now every night. Still, I was able to maintain the same hectic schedule of seeing people with similar problems. In a crazy sort of way I was probably even more effective in helping them through their challenges. After all, I could relate.

"However, I was becoming more isolated and aloof. I certainly wanted to escape, but I didn't know how. I was slowly deteriorating in body and soul, perched on the precarious edge of emotional exhaustion. My marriage stayed together because my wife never left me, although it was an option she had many reasons to choose. We were two well-educated, sincere young people who were putting ourselves through a refining, fiery furnace of chaos that would ultimately help shape us into the persons we were designed by God to be. But burning out the dross, the misplaced ego, and my desire to be a little god was difficult and painful. There were times when I feared the anger of my wife toward me—and God—would push her over the edge. Thank God that didn't happen. But it was a close call."

Can you relate to some of the stress and the denial of stress about which Dan has been talking? Do you sometimes feel that you must manage it all, feel it all, be responsible for it all, and out-perform others as you do it all? At times do you isolate yourself from others and engage in activities such as drinking, overeating, or overshopping that keep you separate, alone, and aloof from friends, colleagues, and people who honestly care about you? Is it becoming harder for you to get up in the morning? Do you frequently burst into tears, not knowing why? Do you feel there's never enough time to finish your work?

If your answer is *yes* to some of these questions, you are not alone. Millions suffer from ulcers, high blood pressure, tension, and addictions brought on by an inability to work through stress and recognize burnout before it starts to take its terrible toll on their lives. The cover of an issue of *Newsweek* reads: "EXHAUSTED: How to spot the danger signs." Inside, the article begins: "We're fried by work, frazzled by the lack of time. Technology hasn't made our lives better, just busier. No wonder one quarter of us say we're exhausted. We need to chill out before we hit the breaking point."[1]

The need to chill out. Good idea. What sensible person would argue with that counsel? But how to do it? Where's the magic pill?

You don't have to be an air-traffic controller, lawyer, NFL football coach, cop on the beat, or the President of the United States to have stress. We all have it. But stress isn't what hurts, maims, and kills; it's how you and I handle it—before it becomes exhaustion. And that's what this book is all about.

Let's go back for the rest of Dan's story.

"I just could not figure out how to start feeling good. I had passed burnout and had moved on to emotional exhaustion. I went to several doctors who put me on antidepressants and other drugs that simply masked my symptoms. It was the classic story of knocking on all the right doors but never receiving the right kind of help. I knew I needed to take control of my life, but doing it was a joke. Most days, I used up the full amount of my energy just to breathe.

"On those days when I had my wits about me, I knew the alcohol that had become my friend was a faulty mechanism for coping with my stress. I was also aware that I wasn't eating properly, wasn't getting enough sleep, and was in a state of constant denial. Then it hit me: *I was also dying spiritually.* My love for God and the church was gone. Fellowship with other Christians meant nothing to me. I made sure I kept myself at a safe distance from those who might help me. I had to have my father intervene in helping me with my bookkeeping; I couldn't even trust myself with my checking account. Without my father's wise, practical counsel, I'm sure I would have been ruined financially. I had become incapable of making the most insignificant personal business decision.

"I knew if I didn't do something fast, it would be all over: business, marriage, and all my personal dreams for success. That's when I finally decided to get help—not from a bottle of pills or alcohol but from those who still loved me enough to hang in there with me.

"Once again I started to believe what I had been telling my clients for years: No one can make you happy without your approval.... If you believe that God is dead, something in you no longer lives.... Evil takes hold when self-neglect takes root.

"My road back to sobriety and emotional well-being was not easy, and I assure you it didn't happen overnight. It took time, prayer, energy, the love of a faithful—although often angry or distraught—wife, and the undying compassion of a merciful God. But eventually I was able to put the pieces back together and regain control of my life."

Why do I tell you Dan's story? Certainly not because he was proud of the fires he put himself and his wife through. If anything, it embarrasses him to tell it. But I have his permission because he hopes his tale of pain and denial will help someone else. This story is important as we begin this book, because it can serve as a touchstone for you, regardless of your situation, to help you do what is necessary to learn to become strong again.

From Burnout to Exhaustion

Perhaps you are a single mother who's working full time. Your kids are with a babysitter or in day care all day. You feel angry, bitter, guilty. Or maybe you're a pastor or youth worker in a church. You spend every hour serving God, loving people, and making a difference in the lives of others. Yet your own marriage is a disaster. You've lost the art of communication with your spouse. *Passion* is only a word in the dictionary. You're ready to call it quits.

Perhaps you've gained thirty pounds over the last year, and you've finally admitted that food is your only true friend. You may have a problem with drinking, or are afflicted with a sexual addiction, or find yourself emotionally or physically abusing others. Whatever your challenge may be, it has you in a vice grip from which you can see no escape. One thing for sure: You are exhausted. Each day is another twenty-four hours of pain and struggle. You scream inside but no one can hear you.

Perhaps you're a teacher, engineer, counselor, factory worker, doctor, computer expert, or lawyer. Regardless of who you are, this book is for you.

When our lives start to sputter and we forget to follow our dreams, we tend to become stagnant. We stop thinking, caring, observing, and reaching out to others. This is usually subtle, but it's the first critical stage of coming distractions. Because of this stagnation and cessation of emotional growth, we stop giving our bodies and minds the proper stimuli they need.

Fear, feelings of guilt, animosity, an unforgiving spirit, loneliness, frustration, or a Lone Ranger mentality can siphon off our energy, potential, and zest for life. Left unresolved, these attitudes develop a life of their own, creating stress that over time can lead to emotional exhaustion. Thoreau once said that most people "live lives of quiet desperation." They look good on the outside but internally they are a seething mass of pain and fear, walking a tightrope of emotional instability, hoping against hope that no one removes the safety net, because they know they are heading for a fall. Until this quiet desperation is dealt with, the exhaustion will remain, and there will be little hope for inner healing.

What do we do when life seems hopeless or out of control? We move into areas we think will help: more work, more alcohol, more obsessive/compulsive activity, more entertainment, more frantic escape from reality. But it's always more and more of the wrong thing. Instead of helping us regain control of our lives, it produces an internal environment that evolves into *burnout*. We feel an uncontrollable sense of disease, but because we're on a vicious cycle of unproductive activity, we keep doing the same unproductive activity over and over. When our burnout and stress builds to a level at which we cannot endure the pain any longer, we cross the line to physical and mental *exhaustion*.

Before long we forget who we are and what we're about. We start to decompose. We no longer feel special. We wonder if God has even taken away our giftedness. We look into the mirror, and we don't like what is looking back at us. We no longer see a beautiful creature, designed in the image of a loving God. Instead, we look through bewildered eyes and see only what is wrong.

We forget that joy comes from within, never from external sources. We fail to remember that spiritual emptiness produces impotence. And because we have selective amnesia of what is truly good, loving, and kind, we become displaced persons, every bit as confused and alone as hapless refugees who stumble onto a foreign shore.

Baby Steps toward Healing

To some degree, we've all been there. We've all broken down in times of weakness. We've suffered, brought pain on ourselves, denied our problems, and refused to seek help—all elements of depression and anxiety. But when we finally reached out for help, we then started to make progress through a series of baby steps that put us on a path of hope, health, and happiness. If you have never walked that path, this is the time to start.

Because I have been hopelessly weak in so many areas of my own life and at times have not accessed the power of God when I needed him most, I feel I can walk with you in your weakness. Just as it's difficult to know *black* if you've never seen *white*, I know what *strong* is because I once lived so long with *weak*. Please don't misunderstand. I have not arrived; I've learned through years of experience that a healthy person is a growing person. So gather your courage to follow in the steps of many others, and do the hard but worthwhile work that will help lead to your own hope and healing.

This healing begins when we finally believe in our heart that we are God's children and that he loves us more than we will ever know. We need to start by getting rid of all the killers of our mind, body, and spirit: the junk food, the negative thinking, the lack of faith in a loving God, the alcohol, the acceptance of abuse. We will need to relearn how to reach out to people, how to be involved in our church, how to slow down, and how to remember that you and I are not asked to play the role of God in any way, shape, or form. Baby steps are required. They are the all-important steps toward inner healing.

You Can Become Strong Again

Do you truly want to be free from emotional exhaustion? If your answer is *yes*, the path leading to this freedom may be the greatest challenge of your life. It will take more than positive thinking, more than reading a book or two, and more than a couple hours of counseling. We are talking about exposing your whole being—the physical, spiritual, and mental—to a lifesaving experience that will help you renew your strength so that you will be able to "soar on wings like eagles . . . run and not grow weary . . . walk and not be faint" (Isa. 40:31). But you may think you barely have the courage, strength, or will to turn the next page, and I'm talking about flying like eagles, running some kind of a marathon, and not fainting. That's right, because you must start where you are. And having just enough strength to turn a page is enough strength to begin.

The good news is that you *can* find healing. Together, we will work hard on ways for you to be able to care for yourself as never before. Your spirit will lift as you develop a plan to work through your challenges, because you will know you're moving toward hope.

If you want to regain control of your life, there are certain things you must do. To become physically fit, you must exercise; to learn a skill or be successful in a specific task, you must practice. The same is true for becoming strong again. There are steps to take. These may not always be obvious. That's because they are often only simple baby steps.

You will have to start with honesty. When you are honest about your problem and your desire to change, you can go on to the next baby step, allowing for help. That can be followed by creating a plan.

If you're in the fire now and you stay in the fire, you will be consumed. However, if you are willing to work through the challenges that face you, then the fire that seems to be singeing your soul will also have the power to purify and refine.

Samuel Butler once wrote, "Life is like playing a violin in public and learning the instrument as one goes on." I'd like to pretend that statement is not true, but I'm afraid it's validated by the history of mankind. The good news here is that starting right now you no longer need to go through it alone. You can draw on the experience and strength of those who have been where you are and know what you are going through. So let's begin our journey toward healing and ask a loving, merciful God to give us the insight and the wisdom to do the right thing.

2

The Long Journey
from Darkness to Light

*God, give us the grace to accept with serenity the things that
cannot be changed, courage to change the things which should
be changed, and the wisdom to distinguish the one from the
other.*

Reinhold Niebuhr

Life is tough. It's easy to talk about how to deal with the
messy stuff of life when things are going reasonably
well—when the bills are paid, when the kids aren't
screaming, when your marriage is thriving, when *stress* is
only a word in the dictionary, when your favorite team is on
a winning streak, and when you don't have to look straight up
to see bottom. But it's another thing when you find yourself
head-to-head, nose-to-nose (sometimes bloodied) with a
person or event that just about destroys you and your self-
esteem.

Who likes to get stressed out, beat up, and burned out
and slink around emotionally exhausted? Not you. Not me.
Then why is it we set ourselves up for so much anguish and

misery? Is there something in our emotional DNA that puts us on a path leading nowhere with people we can't relate to and a future that never quite seems to materialize? This darkness of the soul is what keeps us frantic and emotionally exhausted—especially if we do not take a serious look at what might be the cause of our despair.

A Problem of Self-Esteem

In his landmark book *Modern Times*, author Paul Johnson talks about a short Russian leader whose name was Josef Stalin.[1] To add to what Stalin himself perceived as an all too diminutive stature (five feet four inches), he was also disabled with a stiff left elbow and slightly misshapen hand, which had resulted from an early childhood accident. Further, he was thin, swarthy, and plagued with a pockmarked face. But he was a leader, and he made sure his subjects saw him at his physical best.

When Stalin commissioned his official portrait, he gave strict instructions to the court painter, Nalbandian, to paint him from below—a perspective that would create the illusion of Stalin towering mightily over anyone who viewed the painting. To add to his image of power, the Russian dictator folded his hands across his stomach, making them appear firm and strong like the pseudonym he had chosen, since *Stalin* means "man of steel."

These machinations did make Josef Stalin look good, but they could not improve his self-esteem. Those who knew him said Stalin suffered bitterly from his disabilities and whatever real or imagined intellectual incapacities he may have had. But it was more than an inner fear. Stalin lived out the anger against himself by taking revenge on everyone and anyone with higher capacities. By his fiftieth birthday, he had caused the death of five million peasants and had sent away twice that number to languish in forced labor camps.

Thankfully, the vast majority of people with self-esteem problems do not go on murder binges, become serial killers, or move into positions of power that focus on the physical destruction of others. That's the good news. However, not unlike Josef Stalin, many of us do use physical and emotional cosmetics in an attempt to cover the deeply rooted deficiencies we harbor about ourselves. Why? Because we all want to look good. And why not? Certainly the multibillion-dollar worldwide cosmetics industry continues to count on our desire to cover our blemishes and hide our scars. It's okay to look good and feel good about our appearance, but self-acceptance must come first.

Out of the Darkness

How much of our behavior is healthy, and how much is based on a need for being perfect? To what extent do we allow others to determine our value? When we experience times of stress and exhaustion that assault our self-esteem, we can either rely on an inner reserve to meet our challenges, knowing that God loves us, or we can deny our sense of inner worth, choose to believe that we *are* worthless, refuse to deal honestly with our inner challenges, and adopt behaviors that do not deal with the core problem but help us temporarily feel good about ourselves.

How do we get from the darkness of despair into the light of hope and a future worth striving for? Are there any lasting solutions to these attacks on our self-concept? It is possible to keep our equilibrium when outside forces encroach on us and our personal world is on the verge of collapse! There are ways to cope with these pressures. We can stay on track and create a way of life that will keep us from floundering in anguish and regret. This is a book of solutions.

For Honor and Recognition

In 1900 British Antarctic explorer Sir Ernest Shackleton placed the following advertisement in the newspapers of London, England, as he made initial preparations for his National Antarctic Expedition:

MEN WANTED FOR HAZARDOUS JOURNEY. Small wages, bitter cold, long months of complete darkness, constant danger, safe return doubtful. Honor and recognition in case of success.

Ernest Shackleton

The explorer later said of his call for these intrepid volunteers that "it seemed as though all the men in Great Britain were determined to accompany me, the response was so overwhelming."

Undoubtedly the men of England in the early 1900s who responded to Shackleton's ad already had sufficient challenges in their lives. They surely had their share of economic problems, family difficulties, the stress of being overworked, and all the other issues that are common to us today. Still they responded by the thousands to the call to "small wages, bitter cold, constant danger," and other physical trauma that at any other time would have been considered unreasonable in the extreme.

So why did they say *yes* to Shackleton? It was not because they loved pain—they already had plenty of that. My guess is that they were moved by the last seven words in the Shackleton advertisement: "Honor and recognition in case of success." The would-be adventurers were willing to endure whatever pain might come their way if there could be some assurance that it would have meaning—that they would be doing something important. They were willing to take unprecedented risks, knowing their noble efforts held the potential for some degree of deep, inner reward.

Your Life Script

What is your direction in life? Do you see yourself as simply another cog in the mad machine of random existence, or do you view yourself as someone of great value? What do you believe about God, about yourself, and about the place you hold in your world? Perhaps you have forgotten who you really are. Maybe you've never known. No one wants to live with pain piled on pain, stress layered on stress if there is a deep-rooted sense that life is going nowhere. You may be in such a downward spiral that you wonder if going on is worth the effort.

What causes a negative image of yourself? Your life story holds some valuable clues to solving this mystery.

I remember being terrified by math classes during my junior high and high school years. I can still hear two of my teachers say, "Gregg, you are just no good in math. You won't make it. Better choose a career that does not involve math."

Oh that hurt, and the pain continued for years. Even in college I lived with an unnecessary fear of mathematics. I almost didn't enter the field of counseling because I knew I'd have to take statistics.

Then one day the tutor I'd hired to help me with my college math said I was okay, that I didn't even need a tutor, that I could handle this on my own. Wow, what a relief—and he was right. From that point on, I began to do well in math-related studies. But what a long, painful wait before I gave myself permission to do so.

Think back to your own past. What do you remember that may have blocked you from feeling good about yourself? Perhaps it was a teacher, a parent, a pastor, a Sunday school teacher, a coach, or your peers. Have you lived with the mis-belief that you were not worthy or not good at something and, therefore, did not have much personal value? Perhaps we've all been there. We were not given the freedom to spread our wings, and, therefore, we've spent much of our lives not being the persons a loving God designed us to be.

An important step in regaining control of your life is to understand your life script. Write your personal history in a journal or tell it to a trusted friend. Who are you? Tell the stories of your childhood. Talk about your parents, your grandparents, your great-grandparents. Who were your idols? What did you hate? Whom did you respect? Was it a saintly aunt? A teacher in the third grade who made you feel special? Was it your father or mother?

The Greek philosopher Socrates reminded his disciples that the unexamined life is not worth living. What do you see as you examine your own life? It's important to pay attention to your life script because what you were told to do, to be, to feel, not to do, not to be, not to feel, and how to react have all been the ingredients that have scripted your life. Much of what you learned was good, useful, important. There's nothing wrong with learning to put your napkin on your lap, keep your elbows off the table, and say *thank you* when someone gives you a gift or does something for you. These are all admirable, important qualities for civilized living.

However, you also received other messages that were not as positive. You may have witnessed or been a victim of emotional or physical abuse or neglect.[2] You may have learned early on that you needed to take care of people for your own emotional survival and thus feel you must rescue others to be liked or noticed. You may have been overmothered and underfathered and, therefore, live your life seeking the approval of the opposite sex. Or you may have grown up without a father at all and still carry the terrible pain of a father-shaped vacuum. You may attempt to compensate for past emotional losses by becoming an acceptance junkie

It is possible to restructure the programming that has been carved into our memory banks. Will it be easy? No. Can it be done? I'm confident it can.

through workaholism, overspending, sneaking a drink after work, having an affair, engaging in recreational drugs, or other destructive behaviors.

You may feel vulnerable as you go back through your life script. That's okay, even necessary. But these are important baby steps toward healing. As you search your personal history, fill your mind with the words of Jesus: "You will know the truth, and the truth will set you free" (John 8:32). Jesus knew that truth can never coexist with faulty messages. If you've tried to live with both error and truth, that experience alone has been one of the factors that has set you up for emotional exhaustion.

Most people have not looked deeply enough into their own soul to know their life script is dictating their adult behavior. When life heats up and our stress level elevates to the point of emotional exhaustion, our life script can hurt us. But we can also learn from what has been written on our impressionable heart and begin to change. It *is* possible to restructure the programming that has been carved into our memory banks. Will it be easy? No. Can it be done? I'm confident it can.

Clean Out the Toxic Dump

We all know about the toxic dumps that pose great challenges to our personal health and the environment in general. If there's one near your house or your child's school or playground, you will vigorously protest until it is removed. That's because you know that toxins can slow you down, sap your energy, make you sick, and even kill you. No one in his or her right mind is going to enjoy a stroll in the midst of toxic waste.

Unfortunately much of what has been written in your life script may also be toxic—a belief system that remains filled with confusing, toxic material that does nothing but cause you grief. Because your self-image is the foundation of your personality, it is important to determine what is toxic in your life script and then deal with it.

For example, if you find yourself continually in unfulfilling, unhealthy relationships, I suggest that there is a reason for that hidden in your life script. If you cannot live your life without controlling others, there is something in your life script that continues to feed that frenzy to be the boss at all costs. If you live terrorized by the three potentially deadly emotions of anger, fear, and guilt and you assume the worst is always about to happen to you, you can be sure something in your life script continues to program your adult behavior. If you are abusive to your spouse, colleagues, or children, ask yourself the questions: Where did all that come from? What in my life script could be instrumental in making me the person I am?

Reality Check

We could fill an entire book on the problems we face just in trying to make it from day to day, with sufficient illustrations of pathological personalities to depress us all. Instead, I want us to look at some specific, positive ways to move beyond the prison of the there and then to the excitement of living an emotionally healthy life in the here and now.

First, take a few moments and answer the following questions. Your answers will help you determine whether or not you are living out a previous, largely erroneous life script or whether you are doing a creative rewrite of ancient copy that is more in line with whom you have chosen to become today.

1. Are you weary and tired with your work?
   - Are you drained emotionally?
     yes often sometimes no

   - Do you hate waking up in the morning because you have to go to the same old job again?
     yes often sometimes no

   - Does your work frustrate you?
     yes often sometimes no

   - Do you clash with colleagues at work, often finding yourself at your wit's end?
     yes often sometimes no

   - Do you ever think about death as your only means to escape?
     yes often sometimes no

2. Are you callous toward others?
   - Do you regard others as objects more than people?
     yes often sometimes no

   - Do you have a hard attitude toward colleagues at work?
     yes often sometimes no

- Do you rejoice to see a coworker endure a hardship, especially if you feel that person has wronged you?
  yes often sometimes no

3. Have you thrown away your dreams?
   - Do you blame others for your lack of success?
     yes often sometimes no

   - Have you stopped making plans to do great things with your life?
     yes often sometimes no

   - Do you regard life as little more than a treadmill?
     yes often sometimes no

   - Is life just one big disappointment after another?
     yes often sometimes no

4. Are you an emotional hermit?
   - Do you avoid people who make your life stressful?
     yes often sometimes no

   - Do you feel others drain you and take value from you?
     yes often sometimes no

   - Do you enjoy being the Lone Ranger and a law unto yourself?
     yes often sometimes no

   - Is there any value to you in self-imposed isolation?
     yes often sometimes no

If you answered *no* or only *sometimes* to most of these questions, you are well on your way to living an emotionally fulfilling life. If, however, you said *yes* or *often* to most of the questions, you may well be at some stage of emotional exhaustion. That means you are becoming weaker, not stronger.

These questions lead you to the larger question: Are you getting on with your life with courage and enthusiasm, knowing that somehow you will fulfill your dreams, or have you all but thrown in the towel? Your answers reflect how you see yourself today but they also may suggest that you are still believing and living out too many of the lies your life script may have been feeding you.

Know Your Gifts

The most important message of this chapter is this: You are not flawed because a significant person in your past said you were defective. It doesn't matter if it was a teacher, church leader, family member, or the clerk at the local grocery store. Because you were young, you believed the negative messages you were given. Right now you must ask yourself: Who holds the power over my life today? The answer now is not your teachers, parents, or family members, but the person you see in the mirror. So that's where we need to start, and we must begin by talking about the marvelous gifts God has showered on you—whether you are aware of them or not.

In 1 Corinthians 12:4–7 we read, "There are different kinds of gifts, but the same Spirit. There are different kinds of service, but the same Lord. There are different kinds of working, but the same God works all of them in all men. Now to each one the manifestation of the Spirit is given for the common good."

What do these verses mean and how might they pertain to you and your giftedness? You may protest that you do not have any gifts. Well, I'd have to argue with you about that. You have some wonderful, even tremendous gifts; they just may not look like gifts at the moment. Consider these quite unexpected gifts: God gave Moses a rod, David a slingshot, Samson the jawbone of an ass, Esther the beauty of person, Deborah a talent for poetry, Dorcas the skill to use a needle, and Apollos a tongue of eloquence—and to each the ability to use his or her gift. In so doing, each one of them did effective works for God. But to the casual observer—and to the recipient—they often did not seem like gifts at all.

You may take your gifts for granted and not recognize them because they've always been a part of you. They are the abilities and resources God gave you, perhaps at birth. They are the things you are able to do well, the things that seem to "come naturally" and not require a lot of practice. Other people may recognize your gifts better than you do. Ask three other people what they see as your gifts. You may be surprised at their answers.

I want you to focus on your gifts, because when you are not exercising your God-given gifts, you invariably find yourself out of sync. You struggle to reach your destination, but you're traveling full speed in reverse. You are vulnerable to every slight, and your self-esteem hits rock bottom. If you're not exercising your gifts, you may still be carrying the burdens

---

When you are not exercising your God-given gifts, you invariably find yourself out of sync. You struggle to reach your destination, but you're traveling full speed in reverse. You are vulnerable to every slight, and your self-esteem hits rock bottom.

---

others have placed on your life. Yes, you're still physically alive but you're emotionally exhausted.

There's a story told about Leonardo da Vinci, the famous Renaissance artist. While da Vinci was still a pupil, his old and famous teacher asked him to finish a picture the teacher had begun. Young da Vinci stood in such awe of his master's skill that at first he respectfully declined. But the old artist would accept no excuse. He simply said, "Do your best." Trembling, da Vinci took the brush and began. With each careful stroke, his hand grew steadier as his eye "awoke with slumbering genius." Soon he had forgotten his timidity and was completely caught up in his work. When the painting was finished, the master was carried into the studio to see it. There before him was a triumph of art. Embracing his student, he exclaimed, "My son, I paint no more!"

If Leonardo da Vinci had allowed feelings of inferiority to keep him from painting, the world might have been denied some great works of art. Leonardo's talent surfaced when he did his best with what he had. Doing the best with what you have is all that's required of you. And you will only do your best when you are free to use your gifts as they were intended.

Keys to Success

As you begin to recognize and use your gifts, you will develop a better self-image, higher energy, and increased good humor. Part of developing healthy self-esteem is making a commitment to yourself not to try to please the world. Someone has said that the one magic key to personal fulfillment may be forever illusive, but the sure key to failure is to try to please everyone.

Rather than chasing temporary emotional rewards by playing games with the truth, you can learn to stand up for what you believe, speak the truth in love, live through stormy times with energy and joy, and little by little rewrite your life script. If you wish to live out your giftedness and become strong again—strong enough to take you from exhaustion to emotional health—then it's critical that you make the time to learn and adopt the vital skills of a person with healthy self-esteem.

Eight Traits of Persons with Healthy Self-Esteem

1. *They live with an attitude of humility.* When our gifts and talents are discovered by others, our self-esteem immediately feels the positive thrust of that affirmation.

2. *They speak the truth as they see it, without fear of rejection and with no intent to harm others.* Speaking the truth lovingly is not dependent on whether the recipient is able to hear it. It is never part of our life's assignment to mind other people's business.

3. *They know how to separate feelings from the message being delivered.* Those with good levels of self-appreciation will find it progressively easier to separate emotions from the content of another's communication and will recognize the importance of differentiating between the two in their own communications.

4. *They recognize the role that emotions such as anger, fear, and guilt play in people's lives.* They no longer take their anger, fear, or guilt at face value but instead learn to look beneath the surface to determine the reason for and source of those emotions.

5. *They don't simply follow the followers.* It's like the time-keeper setting his watch by the clock in a jeweler's window so that he can blow the lunch whistle exactly at noon, only to find out that the jeweler was setting his clock by the timekeeper's noon whistle. This is another example of followers following followers.

6. *They look for reasons to* release *others and* believe *in the ability of others to make decisions.* We can help those we love by believing in their abilities and encouraging them to use their gifts. Persons who have healthy self-esteem themselves are better able to respect and appreciate the abilities and skills of others.

7. *They are accountable in word and deed for what they say and do.* Can people count on us when we say we're

going to do something? When we make a promise, do we do our best to keep it? Becoming strong again means taking full responsibility for our actions, which quickly builds self-esteem.

8. *They know the past is the past and the present is the present.* They recognize that to be emotionally healthy they must move from *victim* to *victor.* The strong person with a growing self-esteem is the one who refuses to let the past control what happens today.

Heightened self-esteem comes about by continuing to take those baby steps we talked about earlier, then by making small decisions and seeing small results. As you continue to do this, you will challenge yourself to climb higher mountains and take even greater risks. These are your building blocks to help move you from stress, burnout, and emotional exhaustion to personal freedom and an abundant life.

Never Give Up

To help you make it through the difficult times, it's also important that you make the commitment never to quit pursuing the worthy goal of becoming the person God created you to be. Your ability to withstand the storms of your life will depend on your choice to never give up no matter what challenges may come your way. Reigniting your passion for life requires that you be bold even when you are afraid and courageous even when you feel lost and despairing. As you move beyond your greatest fears to a willingness to allow God to give you the power to make the right decisions, you will find healing.

As you regain control of your life, build your self-esteem, and recover from emotional exhaustion, you will find the strength to keep growing.

- Regardless of how much you may be misunderstood by others, you will keep going.
- When others refuse to appreciate you for your clarity and your frankness, you will not give up.
- When you politely demand the respect of others and don't get it, you will not give up.
- When you speak the truth lovingly, and others reject you anyway, you will not give up.

An unknown author has written a poem that is very appropriate for people recovering from emotional exhaustion and burnout. I have shared this piece in some of my other writings but feel it is worth repeating. You may want to copy it and carry it with you as you take increasing responsibility for your life and move from emotional exhaustion to personal freedom.

You Mustn't Quit

When things go wrong as they sometimes will,
When the road you're trudging seems all uphill,
When the funds are low and the debts are high
And you want to smile, but you have to sigh,
When care is pressing you down a bit,
Rest! if you must—but never quit.

Life is strange, with its twists and turns,
As every one of us sometimes learns,
And many a failure turns about
When he might have won if he'd stuck it out;
Stick to your task, though the pace seems slow—
You may succeed with one more blow.

Success is failure turned inside out—
The silver tint of the clouds of doubt—
And you never can tell how close you are,
It may be near when it seems afar;

So stick to the fight when you're hardest hit—
It's when things seem worst that YOU MUSTN'T
QUIT.

Anonymous

———— *Reflect, Renew, Rebuild* ————

Reflect. As soon as possible, take a ten-minute walk and reflect on the many wonderful things, people, and events you enjoyed as a child. Keep a journal of your thoughts and reflections as you read this book. Start by writing in it two or three of those wonderful things from your childhood. As you write them, ask yourself these two questions:

- What gift or gifts did I use to enjoy my childhood past?
- How might I still use those same gifts today—even in my despair—to affect the life of another human being in a positive way?

Renew. Learn to be your own best friend. You may not always enjoy the luxury of having others near you to give you the lift you need. But with a loving God within, you have all the resources necessary for a full, complete, and satisfying life of love for yourself and of service to others. Keep a self-awareness plan going by maintaining your journal, writing out where you've been, where you are, and where you choose to go. Keep your plan current. Review it and revise it often.

Rebuild. The best diamonds will always be found in your own backyard. It's not necessary to travel far afield to discover the riches of relationships and personal fulfillment. They lie within you, all around you, in your own backyard. All you need is some hard work to dig them up. Write down at least three things that you have access to right now in your own backyard that have the potential to bring strength, joy, and freedom back into your life—things that can take you from darkness into light. These may include favorite books, unfinished projects, crafts, a discussion or Bible study group, or games and sports you enjoy.

3

The Poisons of Anger,
Fear, and Guilt

Holding a grudge causes you to lose your inner beauty.

Gregg Jantz

As we've already seen, when you end up in burnout and emotional exhaustion, there is a slow erosion of your energy and vitality. You seem to be going along reasonably well and then you start to feel a vague sense of disease about some important aspect of your life. Problems you once handled readily are now a pain, and you have neither the time nor the patience to deal with them. Your self-confidence shrinks; you are afraid of difficult tasks that you once took in stride. You have a growing sense of guilt—that you're not performing as you should at work or in the home, that you don't spend enough time with the kids, and that you are letting people down. Your guilt is sapping every ounce of your strength. You are headed on a downward spiral, and in your heart you know if you don't do something about it soon, it will be too late.

Locating the Source

Are you aware that what you are feeling as burnout and emotional exhaustion are really only the tip of a much deeper iceberg? Would you like to get to the source of your problem? Would you like to be able to throw your whole self into your life—like you did when you were a kid—free of anger, fear, and guilt? Are you ready to prepare yourself to smile, laugh, praise others, relax, and let your heavenly Father speak to you in fresh, new ways?

If you really want to work at this, then first I'd like you to answer some simple questions.

1. Do you find yourself waking up some mornings afraid to face the day?

   yes no

2. Would you describe yourself as a person who has peace of mind?

   yes no

3. Do you find it difficult to forgive others?

   yes no

4. Do you ever deny your anger—perhaps because you do not know how to handle it?

   yes no

5. Have you ever paid the price for getting even with someone?

   yes no

6. Do you feel fearful of things, people, or events that are now history?

   yes no

7. Are your fears, for the most part, realistic?

    yes no

8. Do you live with guilt for things that were not your fault?

    yes no

9. Is there something that's making you feel especially guilty at this moment?

    yes no

10. Do you feel you have the ability to choose anger, fear, or guilt in a given situation rather than just accept that emotion as it comes?

    yes no

What do your answers to these questions say about you and where you find yourself at this moment? If you are feeling stressed to the point of burnout or on the threshold of emotional exhaustion, your answers may provide clues to what's going on inside. As you reconsider each question, you may find that anger, fear, or guilt are burdening your life and adding to your stress.

Every day we find ourselves confronted with overbearing, domineering colleagues, neighbors, and even family members who make unreasonable demands on our time, try our patience, and drive us crazy. They seem intent on lowering our self-esteem. They appear as wolves in sheep's clothing, bullying us, forcing us to take more than our share of aspirins, driving our blood pressure sky high, making us bitter, withdrawn, and sometimes even crippling us emotionally.

So we get angry—a natural response to hurt and intimidation. But then we often become fearful, wondering if we've done the right thing by expressing our rage. After all, now we may have really opened Pandora's box. So we back off, hide, or even deny our anger, become a captive of our fears, and begin to live with guilt for having taken a stand in the first place. It seems that we're always living with the big three: anger, fear, guilt.

Does any of this sound familiar? These are normal emotions, but there are times when our anger, fear, and guilt are *not* appropriate—when we hang onto them long after they should have done their useful work. In this chapter we'll see how this contributes to our stress, which can lead to burnout and then to emotional exhaustion. This is when fear, anger, and guilt become emotionally and physically toxic. It's important to know the difference between healthy and unhealthy anger, fear, and guilt, because how you handle these three often poisonous emotions will be a major key to your regaining control of your life.

Anger

If someone steals your wallet, you feel anger. If you come home after a much-deserved vacation and discover your house has been ransacked and burglarized, you feel violated and angry. If someone says something insulting to a member of your family, your anger may be so intense that you want to punch that person in the mouth. These are all understandable emotional responses. You would hardly be a responsible human being if you allowed these events to pass as if nothing had happened.

The Poisonous Nature of Anger

During World War II, the U.S. submarine *Tang* surfaced under cover of darkness to fire on a large Japanese convoy off the coast of China. Since previous raids had left the American vessel with only eight torpedoes, the accuracy of each shot was absolutely essential. The first seven missiles were right on target, but when the eighth was launched, it suddenly deviated and headed back at their own ship. The emergency alarm to submerge rang out, but it was too late. Within a matter of seconds, the U.S. sub received a direct hit and sank almost instantly.

Modern medicine now has documented proof that emotions such as bitterness and anger can cause headaches, backaches, allergic disorders, ulcers, high blood pressure, and heart attacks.

No one could see the torpedo, but it was still coming. It was submerged, hidden, and designed to strike the enemy in secret. But something went terribly wrong, and instead of hitting its intended target, it became a boomerang, coming back to strike the crew that launched it.

There's a lesson here. In this same way, we are also capable of doing irreparable damage to ourselves while we're intent on attacking others. The missiles of anger and hate that we launch will return to hurt us every time. If you read the newspaper, you are aware that people everywhere are destroying themselves and the world in which they live. Yet we do not seem to do the hard work of changing ourselves enough to find inner healing. Modern medicine now has documented proof that emotions such as bitterness and anger can cause headaches, backaches, allergic disorders, ulcers, high blood pressure, and heart attacks. Anger can be a poison, and it can kill.

How to Fight the Fire of Anger

Although modern fire fighting methods have made the old bucket brigade obsolete, the fundamental theory of putting out a fire remains unchanged. To extinguish a blaze you must remove one of the essential elements needed for combustion.

For example, the elimination of fuel is a method often used in fighting a forest fire. A controlled backfire is started from a cleared line ahead of the advancing flames. When the two fires meet, no timber is left to burn. The same principle applies to quenching the flames of anger when the anger is uncalled for, inappropriate, and a hazard to your physical and emotional health. The fuel for inappropriate anger is the wrong beliefs about someone's words or actions and how they affect you. By trying to look beneath the surface of the situation, understanding the other person's motivation and your reactions, you may be able to put out the flame of your self-destructive anger.

Not long ago John came to see me. He was a professor of sociology. Brilliant, astute, popular with students, gifted—this is how his friends described him and his scholastic abilities. For fifteen years John had done careful research on the inner workings of the human psyche. John seemed to know everything one would need to know about human behavior.

However, John's inner life was a tangled web of misbeliefs, misconceptions, misunderstandings, and unresolved anger. How did he know? His stomach told him so every day as he nursed a peptic ulcer that defied medical treatment. Try as he might, John's academic qualifications had not helped him solve his own problem. Not his Ph.D., his scholastic fame, nor even the international symposia on "Human Beings and Stress" that he gave in Europe each year seemed to help him find inner peace. Instead, he was consumed by unresolved, repressed anger about his boyhood. His primary issue was that he felt he had been unfairly treated by his parents, especially since he was convinced they always loved his sister more than they loved him.

If life were theory, John would be able to counsel himself into health. He knew plenty of academic ways to untie his own knotted existence, so he should have been able to find peace based on knowledge alone. But life is not theory, and to know is not necessarily to do. Unresolved anger was tearing John apart.

John had to start looking at his belief system if he was ever going to find inner healing. I had him write down what he finally determined were his wrong beliefs, and several sessions later I asked him to write the truth as he was beginning to see it. Here's what he wrote:

Wrong Beliefs	Truth
I had a miserable childhood, and my problems are primarily due to my parents. I know my folks loved my sister more than they loved me. I just can't forgive them.	I was actually fortunate to have a loving mother and father. I was too young to understand much of what they did. Yes, they may have favored my sister at times, but upon reflection, I know they deeply loved me, too.
It's impossible for me to be happy today because of my unhappy past. I just have too great a backlog of sadness.	I'm smart enough to know that I can't change my past any more than I can change the color of my eyes. I guess I need to make a decision to live life happy or angry. I'm choosing happy from now on.
I have every right in the world to be angry and stay angry if I want to. In fact I really can't change anyway.	I have a God-given right to be angry at injustice, unfairness, and acts that abuse the rights of others. But I do not have a right to suck my thumb and keep demanding my own way at the expense of others. I've been acting like a child for too long, and I'm not going to do it any longer.
It's perfectly all right to demonstrate my anger by throwing things, being late to appointments, and staying steamed up if I want to. Everyone else gets angry; why should I be any different?	I know I can live a much happier life when I ask God to control my actions, my tongue, and my response to frustrating situations at work and at home. From this day forward, I will not selfishly demand things for myself but will begin looking more and more toward the needs of others.

It took time for John to be willing to do this exercise. But once he did, he began the healing process of taking the poison out of his anger and replacing it with love, compassion, and an awareness of the needs of others. His stress is dissipating, and he is on the path to becoming strong again.

If, like John, you have unresolved anger, bitterness, and perhaps a long-standing feud with someone you once cared for, I must tell you frankly that you will remain weak and in-effective in most areas of your life—and I don't think you want to live that way. When you remain angry, you tear down

---

You really cannot afford to keep hanging onto anger and bitterness from the past. You must let it go. Your wound will never heal if you keep opening it up.

---

your self-esteem, fixate on the negatives of life, and create insurmountable roadblocks to your personal, business, and relational success. You are also probably feeling your anger in some part of your body. You really cannot afford to keep hanging onto anger and bitterness from the past. You must let it go. Your wound will never heal if you keep opening it up.

Here is some resentment prevention—four useful ways to rethink your situation when you start to get angry:

1. *Be your own person.* Even if your anger has festered for years, you don't need to let the actions of others dic-tate how you feel. Determine what *you* want out of the encounter. The old idea of counting to ten is still a good rule of thumb before saying anything at all. It will give you time to think about the situation and your response.
2. *Don't intimidate, and don't be intimidated.* Isaiah 1:18 says, "Come now, and let us reason together." What a

great idea. Be assertive by asking the person to be reasonable in your debate, even as you promise to return the favor.

3. *If the shoe fits, wear it.* There may be times when you will be confronted with the truth, but you may not want to hear it. That's when your defenses may rise up like a ten-story building. Again, take a moment and listen to what's being said. If you need time to think about it, say so. Then ask God to give you the courage to accept the truth and confess your fault if necessary.

4. *Practice intentional kindness.* God's Word says that a kind word turns away anger (Prov. 15:1). Think of something positive to say to the person—even if it's, "I hear what you are saying, and I need to take your comments seriously." Take the offensive in praising the accomplishments of others. Edify those with whom you work and live. Tell them when they do good work. Anger and honest praise have difficulty living together. Be known as someone who sees the best in those around you.

Living with bitterness and anger is certain to lead to emotional exhaustion. The good news is that you don't have to tame the tiger of hostility in your strength alone—as we learn in this parable told by David Augsburger:

There was once a tiger keeper and a tiger cub who lived together. The keeper wanted the tiger for a pet, a friend. He fed him, walked him, cared for him. He always spoke softly, warmly to him. But as the tiger grew, his green eyes began to glow with hostility. His muscles rippled their warning of power.

One night, when the keeper was off guard, a lovely girl happened by. The claws reached out. There was a scream. The keeper arrived too late. Then others felt the tiger's teeth—a boy, a man. And the keeper in panic prayed that the tiger might die, but still he lived.

In fear, the keeper caged him in a deep, dark hole where no one could get near. Now the tiger roared night and day. The keeper could not work or sleep through the roars of his guilt. Then he prayed that God might tame the tiger. God answered, "Let the tiger out of the cave. I will give you strength to face him."

The keeper, willing to die, opened the door. The tiger came out. They stood. Stared. When the tiger saw no fear in the keeper's eyes, he lay down at his feet.

Life with the tiger began. At night he would roar, but the keeper would look him straight in the eye, face him again and again. The tiger was never completely in his power, although as years passed they became friends. The keeper could touch him but he never took his eyes off him, or off God who gave him the strength to tame the beast. Only then was he free from the roar of remorse, the growl of guilt, the raging of his own evil.[1]

Fear and Guilt

The twin poisons of fear and guilt have ruined more friendships, wrecked more marriages, damaged more employer/employee relationships, and been at the root of more burnout and emotional exhaustion than most of us are probably aware. But are fear and guilt always harmful?

Fear. When an eighteen-wheeler forces you off a mountain pass and you narrowly escape with your life, adrenaline shoots through your body, your blood pressure rises, and you feel afraid. Or you get a call from the IRS telling you that you will be audited (and please bring your files for the past five years), and you start thinking of every little accounting sin you may have committed—even inadvertently. Your heart begins beating wildly, you start sweating, and you become afraid. Or you learn that a loved one has been in an accident and is barely hanging onto life in the hospital. You become so afraid that you put your life on hold to do what you can to help during that moment of crisis. All are normal responses of fear.

Guilt. Your teenager is living his or her life in a way that's completely the opposite of your values. You can't sleep at night; you're so worried. You know you did your best in raising your child but you find yourself feeling guilty and wondering if you did enough. Or you tell your friend about a business opportunity guaranteed to make you both rich, and the two of you

---

A German proverb says, "Fear makes the wolf bigger than he is." It's also been said, "Fear is tax that conscience pays to guilt."

---

invest heavily in your enterprise. But the deal collapses, you lose a friend, and you both lose your hard-earned cash. You can hardly handle the guilt. After all, it was your fault, wasn't it? Again, normal, human responses to life's twists and turns.

These emotions are normal and necessary, because there are certain things for which we *should* feel fear and guilt. The question is, for how long? "For the guilt-ridden person, death finally becomes an easier option than confession." The late chaplain of the U.S. Senate Richard Halverson said, "Those who fear God face life fearlessly. Those who do not fear God end up fearing everything." A German proverb says, "Fear makes the wolf bigger than he is." It's also been said, "Fear is tax that conscience pays to guilt." Perhaps Corrie ten Boom summed it up best when she said, "The purpose of being guilty is to bring us to Jesus. Once we are there, then its purpose is finished. If we continue to make ourselves feel guilty—to blame ourselves—then that is sin in itself." Corrie is right on the mark—for both fear and guilt.

Taming Our Fear

You and I face fear every day. It may be when we're on the highway, when we're trying to pay our bills, or when our dentist looks in our mouth and says, "Uh-oh!" Many times fear is a flashing light of caution that warns us of imminent danger. This is a fear we've come to trust and appreciate. But what about the times when our fears are terrifying ghosts from a distant past, completely unrelated to today's reality?

You can't do that; you failed once before.

Don't get married again. You botched it up the first time, so what makes you think you'll be successful the second time around?

What, you mean you're going to present that plan to the boss next Monday? Why, you don't have a chance. Don't you remember the last time you tried to make your mark in your company? It was a dead loss.

You say you want to travel to Europe? Why? The skies are filled with terrorists, and you'll probably never make it home.

It's sad that most of us take counsel of our fears, become immobilized by their terror, and seldom become the people God created us to be. We've allowed our fears to fly in the face of our dreams. If this is where you find yourself at this time, I encourage you to pray the following prayer. It helps me whenever I descend into the deep midnight of my own soul.

"Lord, in my darkest hour of fear and anxiety, help me remember that your love casts out fear. Help me to know that there are more people for me than against me and that you want the best for me and my life. Yes, Lord, I am fearful and filled with anxieties, and they are tearing me apart. And to be completely honest, sometimes I even wonder if you are there. You are there, aren't you, Lord? Help me in my fear and in my unbelief. Teach me how to reach out to you, to know I'm not alone, and to never again take counsel of my fears. I know you have already answered this prayer of my heart. Amen."

In an article titled, "Taming Your Fears: Where to Go When Life Gets Scary," Carol Kent writes,

> What happens to us when we experience fear? First, something or someone triggers our fear. It may be a real or an imagined fear. Second, comes my response to the trigger (shock or terror, shame or withdrawal), but fear is what it is really about. Third, we realize our helplessness. We are carried along on an emotional wave—perhaps of rage. Fourth, we feel betrayed. How can this happen to me? How can he or she or life or God let me down so completely?

Precisely. And this is where you and I have a decision to make. We can choose to go it alone, hoping against hope that we'll have the reserve to claw our way out of our own prison of anxiety and despair. Or we can choose a better way, as Carol concludes,

> On the other hand, we can choose the constructive route— to let our raging and thrashing bring us to our knees before God. Like the psalmist who wrote, "When I am afraid, I will trust in you" (Psalm 56:3), we can trust God to take us through whatever lies ahead. In Him we can face the past and accept the truth; we can reveal who we are and not be consumed with shame. I can set my sail, even knowing there will be fearful winds ahead and uncertain rocks beneath the surface.[2]

The Purpose of Guilt—To Bring Us to Jesus

If a crime has been committed, the offender should have a sense of guilt, and the appropriate price must be paid to society. If we have physically or emotionally hurt someone, we need to feel appropriate guilt so we can move on to repentance and receive God's forgiveness.

It's unfortunate, but still true, that so many enter my office day after day to talk to me about years-old guilt-related problems that are not crimes, have not been abusive, and would never have landed them in jail. Still they carry huge millstones of unresolved guilt in their hearts and their bodies. It may be a sense of guilt for something they did in grade school: A thirty-five-year-old woman confessed that she cannot sleep at night thinking about a toy she stole from a local store at the age of ten. Some feel guilty for being too strict with their children or for not being strict enough; for not taking their kids to church at all or for turning them off to the things of God by forcing them to attend Sunday school.

I imagine that as long as we remain human, there will be no end to the things we can feel guilty about. But let's go back to Corrie ten Boom's wonderful quote: "The purpose of being guilty is to bring us to Jesus. Once we are there, then its purpose is finished. If we continue to make ourselves feel guilty—to blame ourselves—then that is sin in itself." A feeling of guilt does not need to stretch into years of unproductive worry, self-recrimination, and anxiety, as if a preoccupation with guilt and remorse could ever change the events of the past.

Guilt is one of our most useless behaviors. Unnecessary guilt is a terrible waste of emotional strength. It saps our courage and makes us weak. This is why the dark recesses of our souls where guilt still lurks must be sanitized and sterilized. Why do we continue to live bound by sins or omissions from the past, when we can live free from their bondage? God has given you and me the excitement of living our lives *today*.

Exorcising Fear and Guilt

The word *should* comes from the Anglo-Saxon word for scold, which is what our *should*s usually do to us. You *should* feel guilty for what you did ten years ago. You *should* remember that God saw what you did. You *should* feel guilty for not earning more money. The rest of this book could be page after page of the scoldings we give ourselves, but what could be more unproductive? We know enough about our problem. So let's deal with this directly. Take out your journal, and write your answers to the following questions:

1. What do I fear most at this time? Where is the *should* in my fear?
2. What does Richard Halverson's statement mean to me? "Those who fear God face life fearlessly. Those who do not fear God end up fearing everything."
3. What one thing do I feel most guilty of right now? Where is the *should* in my guilt?

Don't Give Up on the Wonderful Person God Created

We all make mistakes. Sometimes we fail miserably. We don't keep our promises. We see our lives as land mines of disaster. All this makes us angry, fearful, and ravaged with guilt. Yes, God is your judge, but please don't forget that he is also your forgiver. Your consistency in living a godly life is more important than a single past transgression. So, keeping Corrie ten Boom's comment in mind, when you make a mistake: feel the anger, fear, or guilt, admit it, confess it, make amends, and move on—fast! It's one of the best ways to find inner healing.

Then evaluate your choices, knowing you are forgiven, healed, and whole in God's eyes. Recognize that today is a new day. You have a beautiful, clean, white sheet of paper on which to write a new story of God's love for you. Yes, by the end of the day it won't be so clean; it'll be dog-eared and smudged, and you'll certainly need to ask God for his forgiveness once again. But that's what our Christian faith is all about—to take each day of our lives as yet another opportunity to make the right choice and not wallow in the past, which will only cloud and distort our future.

Failures are events, not people. That's why I hope I can persuade you to be kinder to yourself. To become strong again, you need to move away from your static, overly ordered world and enter the freshness of God's love; open your heart to his unshakable goodness, his forgiveness of your sins, and his redeeming love. Over time, you will say good-bye to the poisons of anger, fear, and guilt, because you will learn to put them to their proper use. And what better time to start doing this than today!

Reflect, Renew, Rebuild

Reflect. God's Word is your personal manual to help you deal with inappropriate anger, fear, and guilt in your life, and the wisdom and comfort of the Psalms is a wonderful place to seek that counsel. As you read these verses, take courage in knowing that as a child of God you no longer need to fear the emotional enemies of your past or your present. Reflect on these words of the psalmist as you inch away from emotional exhaustion and move closer to inner healing.

O LORD, how many are my foes!
    How many rise up against me!
Many are saying of me,
    "God will not deliver him."
But you are a shield around me, O LORD;
    you bestow glory on me and lift up my head.
To the LORD I cry aloud,
    and he answers me from his holy hill.
I lie down and sleep;
    I wake again, because the LORD sustains me.
I will not fear the tens of thousands drawn up
    against me on every side.

Psalm 3:1–6

Renew. People who insist on being rigid and unchanging and who possess little or no desire to grow into the person God created them to be are prime candidates to stay angry, fearful, and guilty—which makes them weak. They choose to live in the dim light of a dismal past. Instead of being forty or fifty years old, many have actually had only one year of experience forty or fifty times.

On the other hand, those refreshing human beings who are open, flexible, and willing to change and who see God's goodness new each day refuse to be so tough on themselves. They no longer bend today's reality to fit yesterday's conclusions. Instead, they review and revise their plans, knowing that God will remain faithful to them to the end.

Here's a verse I would encourage you to memorize as you seek out the desires of your heart: "One thing I do: Forgetting what is behind and straining toward what is ahead, I press on toward the goal to win the prize for which God has called me heavenward in Christ Jesus" (Phil. 3:13–14).

Rebuild. Write a paragraph in your journal stating why you know in your heart that God loves you unconditionally.

Tell your heavenly Father where you've been, where you are now, and what you are prepared to do from this moment on to become strong again. Know that your God loves you with an everlasting love and that you can live with the assurance that he has never failed you and that he did not design you as an anger, fear, or guilt machine but rather as a person created for peace, joy, and abundant life.

4

Forgiveness

The Path to True Intimacy

Belinda: Ay, but you know we must return good for evil.
Lady Brute: That may be a mistake in the translation.

Sir John Vanbrugh

If we want to find inner healing, it's important that we become deliberate in creating healthy relationships—even if we've had unfortunate experiences in our past. None of us can grow healthy alone. We need relationships that are intimate, open, and honest, in which we can be ourselves—unafraid and candid about what's happening in our life. This means we must have an understanding heart and a willingness to forgive each other. Forgiveness is essential in fostering relationships if they are to be healthy and satisfying. Such relationships can help us grow into the people God wants us to become.

Forgiveness has an overwhelming power to do the unexpected. It delivers what is often seen as undeliverable, goes beyond the call of duty, orchestrates a truce to the conflict—and does it with joy. You and I have been at both ends of the spectrum, haven't we? We've been forgiven, and we've been the forgivers. We know what it's like to disappoint a friend, not keep a promise, or cause pain in the heart of someone

---

Those of us who want long, meaningful, intimate friendships will need to develop short memories.

---

we love. For this, we must ask forgiveness. And when on the receiving end of the pain, we know how challenging it can be to forgive someone who has hurt us.

Author Arch Hart reminds us that "forgiveness is surrendering my right to hurt you back if you hurt me," which means that those of us who want long, meaningful, intimate friendships will need to develop short memories, because the art of being a forgiving friend is the art of knowing what to remember and what to overlook.

Learning to Forgive

Without a spirit of forgiveness, we will remain stale, uninteresting, emotionally unattractive people who spend our lives tallying up the sins of others. Once we really get into not forgiving people, there's no end to what we can record. The longer the list grows, the more justified we feel in harboring our resentments. Yes, much of what we record may be painfully true, but of what advantage is it to us to keep such certifiable accounts of wrongs? We become charter members in what I call the *Order of the Clenched Fist*—an exclusive club that chooses neither to give nor receive good gifts.

Have you ever been there? If so, did it make you happy? Was it worth the effort to tally the wrongs of others? Wouldn't it be far better just to let it go and free yourself to reach out for the refreshing and the new? That's what I had to do, and I'd like to tell you my story.

Some years ago, at the peak of my own emotional exhaustion and while in the depths of personal depression, I felt nothing else could happen to make my life any more difficult. Unfortunately, I was wrong. Unknown to us, an employee at The Center for Counseling and Health Resources, Inc., had determined to destroy everything my wife and I together had worked so hard to create. He was maligning us in letters and in personal contacts with our clients. He took important documents out of his personnel file, stole proprietary information from The Center, and was preparing to establish a base for a future, competitive operation in the same area.

When I finally discovered what was happening, I was livid but too emotionally exhausted from the other challenges I was facing to think creatively about how to deal with this individual—much less think about forgiving him. My fist was definitely clenched. I couldn't believe the damage this once trusted employee was doing to our business and our reputation. In the heat of the moment, it didn't occur to me that the remedy for wrongs is to forgive them. I'd been cheated, lied to, victimized, and hit in the pocketbook. Besides, I had a right to feel that way—right? But the angrier and more out of control I got, the greater my emotional exhaustion. I was being eaten alive by my anger and refusal to forgive.

On the day this person physically left our premises, my wife, LaFon, approached him as he was walking out the door. She looked him in the eye and said, "I don't know all the things you have done to try to hurt us, but I want you to know that I forgive you for everything."

Neither LaFon nor I knew of half the plotting this former employee had done, and here LaFon tells him she's forgiven him. Unbelievable! I was certainly not going to forgive him; I wanted to get even. My angry heart kept saying, *Okay, two can play this game. If you bring me down, I'll bring you down further. You'll never work in this or any other town again.* My blood pressure rose; my heart beat through my chest; my stress level went into the stratosphere; and I doubt if anyone could have measured the intensity of my emotional exhaustion. I had come to the end of my rope, and it was fraying fast.

I'd been a counselor for years, so I knew intellectually that resentment and emotional freedom cannot coexist. I had always counseled clients against hanging onto anger, resentment, and an unforgiving spirit, yet I had to come to the point of complete emotional exhaustion before I could give up my right to get even. I had to pray and act on God's guidance for a forgiveness beyond my own capability that would once again give me the freedom to love.

To recover from emotional exhaustion, we must take honest, often painful, risks in several areas of our lives. The risk we're discussing here is to learn to forgive in order to enjoy relationships that are significant, honest, and intimate. However, if you are like I was, you may be so emotionally exhausted that you can't even spell the word *forgiveness*, much less act in forgiving ways.

If you find yourself burned out, tired, and perpetually drained, there's a good chance you may be trying to go it alone emotionally like I was. I know the pain you are going through, even though I don't know the details of your struggle. It's possible you don't have any intimate friendships. (I define *intimacy* as a nonsexual, honest desire to be open and vulnerable with someone you care about and who cares about you.) If this is your situation, then we need to find a way to move you from the bondage of anger and hurt to the freedom of acceptance, self-approval, and forgiveness. Of the many antidotes for emotional exhaustion we will discuss in this book, the reality of a forgiving spirit is the most important in moving you forward on your pilgrimage to inner healing.

Until I could finally forgive that former employee who had wronged me, I allowed my resentment to develop a destruc-

---

Of the many antidotes for emotional exhaustion we will discuss in this book, the reality of a forgiving spirit is the most important in moving you forward on your pilgrimage to inner healing.

---

tive life of its own. Worse than that, my other relationships suffered along the way. I was holding back from those I cared about, was not being honest with friends, and chose not to tell my most trusted confidants of my fears, hurts, or emotional pain. When I finally asked God to help me forgive, it was as if he turned the light back on in my life.

As we face the challenges of developing healthy relationships, I want you to reflect on the following statements and write your answers in your journal.

1. Being intimate/honest with someone—even for a short time—is difficult for me.
   yes no sometimes

2. I've been hurt before and I don't want to get hurt again. Therefore, I don't choose any degree of intimacy in my relationships.
   yes no sometimes

3. I have difficulty telling even my best friend when I am afraid, hurt, or in emotional pain.
   yes no sometimes

4. I feel if I could learn to relax, begin to appreciate the gifts of others, and have a more forgiving spirit, I would then be on my way to inner healing.

   yes no sometimes

5. Mutual respect, trust, kindness, and honesty are important in relationships, and I would like to have these kinds of friendships in my life.

   yes no sometimes

6. I believe one of the keys to dealing with emotional exhaustion is to take the risk of forgiving others for what they've done to me.

   yes no sometimes

How did you respond? Do your answers help you know where you need to work hardest?

In his wonderful book *Killing Giants, Pulling Thorns,* Charles R. Swindoll writes, "The answer to resentment isn't complicated, it's just painful. It requires *honesty*. You must first disclose and expose the giant. It then requires *humility*. You must confess it before the One who died for such sins. . . . Finally it requires *vulnerability*—a willingness to keep that tendency submissive to God's regular reproof, and a genuinely teachable, unguarded attitude" (emphasis added).[1]

Perhaps a traumatic event in your past has made you afraid of pursuing an honest, intimate relationship again. You say you've been there, done that, and no more, thank you. The only trouble with stubbornly refusing to take the risk of forgiving and moving on is that you get stuck in your hurt and isolation. Barbra Streisand was right when she sang, "People who need people are the luckiest people in the world." Why is this? Because relationships keep us healthy. Only in relationships can we perfect our ability to discern what is good and what is not. You cannot accomplish this goal while sitting all alone nursing wounds of the past. (See chapter 5 for further discussion of ghosts from the past.)

God designed you to be emotionally healthy, and that's why he built a forgiveness factor into your spirit. When you repress your emotions—any of them—your gut keeps score. But when you take the risk of opening up to others and begin to share who you are with someone you learn to trust, you are on your way to emotional wholeness. The good news is that you can learn to use the fear and miscues of your past to carry you high above the turmoil. You can choose to let the real you begin to emerge—that stronger you who chooses to be emotionally exhausted no more.

One of the first things you must do is quit playing the blame game—one of life's greatest emotional handicaps. You must be willing to take responsibility for your own words and actions and allow others to take responsibility for theirs. Listen to what others are saying, but take into account who is speaking. With your Christian brothers and sisters, practice submitting to each other in love.

As you regain control of your life, you substitute personal accountability for blame, love for hate, forgiveness for a spirit of resentment. You finally learn the truth that love refuses to enjoy evil and does not gloat at the sins of another, but instead, forgives—again and again. Love takes full responsibility for its actions and gives up the right to get even.

Be an Ant, Not a Grasshopper

You may remember Aesop's fable about the ant and the grasshopper. While the busy ant was out collecting food all summer, the flighty grasshopper spent his time playing around, smelling the roses, and enjoying his undisciplined life. Then when winter came, the grasshopper was out of nourishment and almost out of luck. He surely would have starved if the friendly ant had not shared some of the food he and his fellow ants had carefully stored up for their own use.

Such are the risks grasshoppers—and people—take who consume without making a contribution. When we refuse to forgive or continually blame others for our problems, we take those same risks, because we are unable to make positive contributions to relationships. Our self-respect demands that we make some contribution to a friendship, even if we begin with baby steps. This is where the inner healing must begin.

When I was finally able to join LaFon in forgiving our ex-employee, I began to find the energy for my own self-care. I gave up my plans for revenge that I was sure would bring my adversary to his knees. But I never could have done it alone. Instead, I broke down and prayed that God would give me his grace to forgive.

Having taken that step, I went back to work at The Center. I quit worrying; I quit playing the blame game; and inner peace finally returned to my life. My stress diminished, and, amazingly, my emotional exhaustion decreased. For a variety of reasons, it was not long before my former employee's newly established counseling practice was closed down, and what seemed to have been a major storm for me turned out to be only a passing squall. I learned a valuable lesson from this: We don't need to bring evil to its knees. Our job is to ask God to make us forgiving, loving persons and let him take care of the rest.

What Forgiveness Does

As a result of this experience with a former employee, I realized we needed to be more careful in our hiring practices

---

We don't need to bring evil to its knees. Our job is to ask God to make us forgiving, loving persons and let him take care of the rest.

---

at The Center, and we made those changes. We altered our organizational structure to become more efficient and built in an accountability component for our counseling team. We became wiser in our business judgment and put in safeguards to prevent any future sabotage of our work. The experience also helped me to grow emotionally with my wife, my friends, and my staff. When I let go of my bitterness, I became emotionally stronger. And this is what can happen to you when you believe in your heart—and act on your belief—that forgiveness is your true path to intimacy, healthy relationships, and inner healing.

Getting Healthy One Day at a Time

When you first attempt to fix your life, the scattered parts may resemble a jigsaw puzzle. The picture is there in front of you but it's in pieces and you must do the hard work of putting it all together. But aren't puzzles more interesting and easier to do when you don't have to work them all alone? That's why you and I need a friend or two with whom we can share our joys and pain. If we allow trusted friends to help us put the pieces back together, we will find the puzzle really gets interesting as the picture develops more color and depth. As we engage life in fresh new ways, we will find we are not so afraid and we are more forgiving of the actions of others. We will feel increasingly confident as we become strong again.

Rigidity versus Flexibility

If you are stiff in your approach to life and so burned out and weary that you insist your puzzle go together immediately, you'll find yourself even more perplexed, tired, stressed, and exhausted. A fear of intimacy in relationships is often a symptom of this rigidity. Putting your life's puzzle together will take time and effort, but to grow into the person you want to become it's critical that you break out of your emotional prison and ask God for the strength you need to take some risks with others.

Your heavenly Father has a few wonderful words for you right now—in case you're not yet convinced this is the way to go. Through the pen of the prophets, God has said to you, "I have loved you with an everlasting love" (Jer. 31:3). "Can a mother forget the baby at her breast? . . . I will not forget you! . . . I have engraved you on the palms of my hands" (Isa. 49:15–16). What an encouraging description of God's love for you—even to his carving your name on the palms of his hands. How graphic. How indelible! This means the God who created the universe is constantly aware of your name

---

God has said to you, "I have loved you with an ever-lasting love" (Jer. 31:3). "Can a mother forget the baby at her breast? . . . I will not forget you! . . . I have engraved you on the palms of my hands" (Isa. 49:15–16).

---

and your concerns. Why would he do this if you did not have immense value to him? Still, you have a choice: You can refuse to accept God's unconditional love or you can embrace it with all your heart, soul, and mind. You can receive his forgiveness or you can choose not to. It's my prayer that you make the right choice and accept his generous offer of unconditional love; then take that love power and share it with others. As you give to those around you, you will be surprised to see how much of your strength returns, how bouts of depression may become a thing of the past, and how your spirit of forgiveness will win the day.

For Men Only

Psychologist Herbert J. Freudenberger suggests that American men are finding their roles and expectations particularly confused as a result of changes in sexual norms, the emphasis on material success, women's liberation, a lack of male intimacy with other males, and a scarcity of mentors. Increasingly, he suggests, men are having trouble with commitment and responsibility in relationships, instead, pouring those values into their jobs. The solution, suggests Freudenberger, lies in first learning to feel secure with themselves, to trust and like themselves. They must examine their priorities, directions, and goals.[2]

Men need to open up to their feelings and discuss their vulnerability and fears. In their relationships, they must develop more realistic expectations and view those relationships as changeable situations where they may encounter both pleasant and unpleasant experiences, both disappointment and joy. To measure a relationship in terms of immediate success is an adolescent approach. Time for relationships has to be built into a man's life. Freudenberger says, "If men begin to recognize that they can gain far more by legitimately caring, loving and collaborating, they may find less need to combat, compete and overpower each other."[3]

Although Freudenberger did not use the word *forgiveness*, I think he would be comfortable adding it to his list of things for men to do. We need to take his perspective seriously, because we men need to learn to be as interested and concerned with who we *are* as with what we *do*.

Women seem to be much better at this, as the bestseller *Men Are from Mars, Women Are from Venus* affirms. So guys, we need to take a few lessons from our wives and significant others—those who are usually more concerned with who they are than what they do. For all of us, to forgive theoretically is not difficult. To forgive for real is the challenge. Perhaps we find it difficult to forgive because we secretly enjoy condemning others. There is some satisfaction in nursing our wounds. As long as I felt comfortable condemning the actions of the one who hurt me, I found it easy to feel superior. I also discovered it was a dead-end way to live. When you and I understand this principle for living, we will cancel the debt and mark the transaction *paid*. Real forgiveness comes, as Dr. Maxwell Maltz says so beautifully, "When we are able to see, and instantly accept, that there is and was nothing for us to forgive" and that we had no right to condemn or hate the other person in the first place.

Six Myths about Intimacy

Both men and women have myths about intimacy. Myths are just that—fairy tales, fabrications. They have a hint of truth but seldom hold up to close scrutiny. Perhaps you have lived with certain dark intimacy myths in the past that now must be exposed to the light of truth. As you now come out of hiding, let's shatter a few of these myths that may have restricted your growth with unrealistic expectations.

1. *You need to be a mind reader.* Nothing is further from the truth. Intimacy is not a mind game. It's about honesty and openness. The greatest thrill comes when you and another person begin to honestly share yourselves with each other.

2. *I can treat you any way I wish.* No one has the right to treat another person as he or she wishes. Perhaps this is what has happened to you in the past, and you have equated past hurt with intimacy. This is emotional abuse, pure and simple. Regard it as such.

3. *Give me a minute, and I can fix you.* We don't need handyman relationships. It's neither our job nor our privilege to fix people or their problems. More lasting results will come about from openness and honesty than from manipulation and looking for what's wrong so we can fix it.

4. *Caring is a feeling.* If this is true, then when you stop caring, the relationship, by definition, must come to an end. When you reach out to a friend or colleague, you do it because that person is your friend, and you reach out whether or not you feel anything. Feelings are nice but they are not the material of which great relationships are made.

5. *You've got to spill all your guts.* This is probably one of the greatest myths of all. The most vibrant relationships are often the quiet ones—walking together on a beach, going to a concert, having a cup of coffee together, or enjoying a simple conversation. There are no *have to*s in a relationship of true intimacy. If anything, *should*s and *must*s will dampen the growth of your friendships quicker than anything else.

6. *It's got to be a good relationship all the time.* This myth is what out-of-touch-with-reality B movies are made of. You live in the real world, and that means you, your

friends, and your relationships will be flawed. Nothing in this life of hills and valleys will stay good all the time. Your relationships must simply be allowed to be. What you see is what you get. Openness, honesty, and intimacy need to be unconditional, for this is the only brand of caring that will bring health and growth to your relationships.

An intimate relationship is one in which there is emotional safety, when you feel understood, accepted, and affirmed. You allow yourself to be vulnerable without the fear that the other person will misuse your trust to hurt you. In this kind of a relationship, you can grow emotionally and spiritually.

Making the Love Chapter Your Chapter

Mother Teresa has long been a wonderful example of God's love. She once said that the aim of her work was to take God, to take his love, to the homes of the poorest poor and to lead them to him. She believed that it made little difference who they were, what their ethnic background was, or what their place in society was. She and her coworkers simply wanted to show others the love and compassion God had shown them.

This is love. This is caring. This is what it means to live a life of forgiveness and withholding judgment—a sure, solid foundation for developing relationships of honesty, intimacy, and trust.

Eleanor Chestnut, a medical missionary in China, was a model of love and forgiveness. A beggar had come to the hospital badly burned, but no one was willing to donate skin for a graft. The next morning the nurses were surprised to learn that the operation had been performed. Then they noticed that Dr. Chestnut was limping and realized that she had surgically removed some of her own skin to save the victim's life. They were amazed at such a sacrifice, for they couldn't understand why she would care so much for a total stranger.

Later, during the Boxer Uprising, this gallant missionary again manifested a selflessness that profoundly impressed the Chinese people. She had been unjustly accused of being a counter revolutionary. Yet, she maintained a spirit of forgiveness even as her captors were removing her from her home. As she was being led to a filthy prison to await her fate, she saw a little boy bruised and bleeding. Immediately she broke away from her captors, and kneeling down she bound up the youngster's wound. A few hours afterward she was executed. More than half a century has now passed, and Chinese Christians and nonbelievers alike still talk about the foreign doctor whose loving concern and spirit of forgiveness made them think of Jesus.

First Corinthians 13 remains the keystone to this kind of love. Even though you've read it a hundred times before, I encourage you to let the words of this passage wash over your spirit. As you read it, ask yourself:

1. Do I have the kind of heart that's prepared to exercise a forgiving spirit?
2. As a result of this forgiveness, am I edging closer to more honest, intimate relations with others?

If I speak in the tongues of men and of angels, but have not love, I am only a resounding gong or a clanging cymbal.

If I have the gift of prophecy and can fathom all mysteries and all knowledge, and if I have a faith that can move mountains, but have not love, I am nothing.

If I give all I possess to the poor and surrender my body to the flames, but have not love, I gain nothing.

Love is patient, love is kind. It does not envy, it does not boast, it is not proud.

It is not rude, it is not self-seeking, it is not easily angered, it keeps no record of wrongs.

Love does not delight in evil but rejoices with the truth.

It always protects, always trusts, always hopes, always perseveres.

Love never fails. But where there are prophecies, they will cease; where there are tongues, they will be stilled; where there is knowledge, it will pass away.

For we know in part and we prophesy in part, but when perfection comes, the imperfect disappears.

When I was a child, I talked like a child, I thought like a child, I reasoned like a child. When I became a man, I put childish ways behind me.

Now we see but a poor reflection as in a mirror; then we shall see face to face. Now I know in part; then I shall know fully, even as I am fully known.

And now these three remain: faith, hope and love. But the greatest of these is love.

—————— *Reflect, Renew, Rebuild* ——————

Reflect. The great English evangelist John Wesley was about twenty-one years of age when he went to Oxford University. He came from a Christian home and was gifted with a keen mind and good looks. Yet in those days he was a bit snobbish and sarcastic. One night, however, something happened that set in motion a change in Wesley's heart. While speaking with a porter, he discovered that the poor man had only one coat and lived in such impoverished conditions that he didn't even have the comfort of a bed. Yet he was an unusually happy person, filled with gratitude to God. Wesley, being immature, thoughtlessly joked about the man's misfortunes. "And what else do you thank God for?" he said with a touch of sarcasm. The porter smiled, and in a spirit of meekness replied with joy, "I thank him that he has given me my life and being, a heart to love him, and above all a constant desire to serve him!" Deeply moved, Wesley recognized that this man knew the meaning of true thankfulness.

Many years later, in 1791, John Wesley lay on his deathbed at the age of eighty-eight. Those who gathered around him realized how well he had learned the lesson of praising God in every circumstance. Despite Wesley's extreme weakness, he began singing the hymn, "I'll Praise My Maker While I've Breath."

What Wesley learned is something we all must accept as gospel truth: All forgiveness begins in our hearts with an attitude of praise and gratitude. Each day we need to make the decision to be thankful for who we are and whatever God has given us.

Renew. One of the best ways to remind ourselves of our goals is to see ourselves already there with daily affirmations. Write the following six affirmations in your journal. Note that the affirmations are all in the present tense, and they are not filled with *maybes*, *shoulds*, or future possibilities. You may want to add to the list. Then repeat each one—two or three times a day. Think forgiving thoughts and you'll become a forgiving person; think thoughts of caring for others and you will be known as a person of compassion.

- I accept the reality that joy comes from within, not from without, and that with God as my source of strength, I assume responsibility for my solutions.

- I am a forgiving, loving person and I enthusiastically embrace others, regardless of what they may have done to harm me.

- I now know that honesty in relationships is what true intimacy is all about. Right now I see myself as an open, caring person who looks to the needs of others more than to my own concerns.

- I know that emotional emptiness can lead to spiritual impotence and I am impotent no more. I am a forgiving, loving child of God who continually looks for the best in others.

- I enthusiastically accept the fact that it's okay to make mistakes, because that means I am growing. I am committed to living and learning and I am doing this by opening myself up to others.

- I am happily asking more from myself than from others. The blame game is over, and my life of forgiving is in full swing. I am a new person, created and designed by my heavenly Father for now and for eternity.

Rebuild. Honesty without deep compassion and unconditional understanding is not honesty at all but subtle hostility. Would you agree? As you begin to rebuild your own spirit and become a more forgiving person, what are you prepared to do today to put what you are learning in this chapter into action? (Perhaps you need to make a phone call, write a letter, stop by to see a friend.) Give yourself a precise time by which you will complete your commitment and write it in your journal.

5

Removing the Ghosts
from Your Past

*Unfriendly ghosts from your past may never disappear
    entirely.
They can return to haunt you at a moment's notice.
The key is to keep meeting these apparitions head-on,
remembering they are as cold as last winter's hearth,
and need have no bearing on your life today.*

Robert C. Larson

As a result of a damaging brain fever at the age of
nineteen months, Helen Keller was deaf and blind,
communicating only through hysterical laughter or
violent tantrums. Nevertheless, with the help of her teacher,
Anne Mansfield Sullivan, Helen learned to read braille and to
write by using a special typewriter. Their early relationship
was the subject of *The Miracle Worker*, a 1960 Pulitzer prizewinning play and 1962 film by William Gibson.

In 1904 Helen Keller graduated with honors from Rad-
cliffe College and began a life of writing, lecturing, and fund-
raising on behalf of the handicapped, becoming one of the

most inspirational women of all time. Her life is one example after another of what it means to become strong in the midst of unrelenting difficulty, stress, and pain.

At the close of her autobiography Helen Keller writes,

Fate—silent, pitiless—bars the way. Fain would I question his imperious decree; for my heart is undisciplined and passionate, but my tongue will not utter the bitter, futile words that rise to my lips, and they fall back into my heart like unshed tears. Silence sits immense upon my soul. Then comes hope with a smile and whispers, "There is joy in self-forgetfulness." So I try to make the light in other people's eyes my sun, the music in others' ears my symphony, the smile on others' lips my happiness.[1]

When we feed our faith, we starve our doubts. That's what Helen Keller did for an entire lifetime, and it is what you and I must do if we are to find inner healing. It's easy to lament the past, play the role of victim, live with *if onlys*, and be consumed with profound doubts about our present and future based on earlier trauma. I know how easy it is, because I've been there all too often. We all have people, events, and memories in our background that haunt us, confuse us, and throw us for a loop at the most unsuspecting moment. We may be at a Christmas concert where we hear the choir sing, "I'll Be Home for Christmas," and we well up with tears knowing we will never go home again under any circumstances. Or we may see a couple holding hands walking a deserted beach at sunset, and we recall a day when we were in a loving relationship that is no more.

There's no end to the fuel we could use to feed our sadness, fears, and doubts. But permitting the ghosts of our past to have a life of their own today will not help us recover from emotional exhaustion. In this chapter you will find some things to do to take yourself a few steps farther down the road to freedom from past hurts and memories as you rid the past of its emotional poison, learn from its lessons, and use what

---

There's no end to the fuel we could use to feed our sadness, fears, and doubts. But permitting the ghosts of our past to have a life of their own today will not help us recover from emotional exhaustion.

---

was once negative energy to press on with your new life as you become strong again.

Failure Is Never Final

In the world of business the name Charles Schwab is legend. Charles Schwab & Company is the world's largest and most innovative discount brokerage house. *Fortune* magazine dubbed Schwab "the king of discounting." With 235 branch offices worldwide and more than ten thousand employees, 1995 revenues broke records at $1.42 billion, a 33 percent gain over the year before. Not bad for someone from California's San Joaquin Valley who, as a little boy, struggled to read a simple sentence.

As a child, Charles Schwab had to work harder in school than his fellow classmates, although he didn't know why until the mid-1970s when his ten-year-old son Michael was diagnosed with dyslexia, a learning disorder that makes reading excruciatingly difficult. That's when Charles realized that dyslexia was his problem as well. Schwab has said that if it weren't for the *Classics Illustrated* comic series, he wonders if he would have made it through school. His teachers assumed he was slow, so Schwab believed it.

What might have been a curse to some became a blessing in disguise to Charles Schwab, because it allowed him to see the world differently. While those around him received better grades, moved throughout society with greater ease, and climbed up the academic ladder more quickly, Schwab had to look at the world differently to survive. Many of his contemporaries were able to get by observing only what was immediately in front of them. Even while attending Stanford University, his reading speed was about half that of the average Stanford student. Just as he'd relied on the *Classics Illustrated* comic series as a child to get him through grade school, he now relied on *Cliff Notes* to help him get through Stanford.

Schwab had learned something we all must learn if we want to overcome emotional exhaustion. He refused to allow a disability or the frustration of a handicap to slow him down, make him weak, or bank the fires of his dream. What could have been a daunting ghost from Schwab's past—fertile ground for unresolved stress and emotional exhaustion—instead became good soil where he drove down roots that resulted in unprecedented business success.

Perhaps you can relate to Schwab's challenges in one way or another. Are there ghosts in your past (people, ideas, or events) that keep tying you in knots, preventing you from becoming the person you know God wants you to be? Do you feel isolated or distrust other's intentions because you've been hurt before? Are you using the past as an excuse for failure or are you turning former trauma into positive energy to become strong again?

Do you desire to have the freedom to feel better about yourself and to live in joy and peace? Your ability to become strong again has much to do with whether you live confidently in the present or as a victim of your past. You can learn proven principles to help you change the *perception* of your past and begin to use your life experience as a vehicle for growth.

Revisiting the Past

Just as your friendly neighborhood realtor reminds you there are only three things to consider when buying a home—location, location, location—so it is with your new way of looking at the past. It's perspective, perspective, perspective. If we can revisit our past and see old events with adult eyes, we will take a big step toward inner healing.

Lessons from Dodge City

I was raised in Dodge City, Kansas. Located on the Arkansas River, Dodge City was settled in 1872 and soon became a notorious frontier town and cattle-shipping point on the Santa Fe Trail and the home of Bat Masterson. One of the legendary gunslingers of the nineteenth-century American West, Masterson was a scout, Indian fighter, buffalo hunter, and railroad worker before he became deputy sheriff of Dodge City in 1876.

Of course, all this was long before my arrival. By the time I was born, Dodge City was actively reliving its legendary past. The Arkansas River still flowed through the center of town, and as a child, I thought it was the largest, longest, most dangerous body of water on earth. The Old West buildings on Front Street also seemed enormous to me—soaked with the blood of past gunfights and housed with the ghosts of ne'er-do-wells still pulling six-shooters from their holsters, gunning down the good guys. Boot Hill was still there—yet another reminder of where a person would be sure to end up if he wasn't quick on the draw. To a child, Dodge City was bigger than life: big river, big streets, big buildings, bigger-than-life cowboys. But were they really all that big?

Then I remember the first time I returned home as an adult. I went down to the Arkansas River and thought, *What's so big about this trickling body of water? In the state of Washington we'd call it a stream.* Then I walked over to Front Street and thought, *It's interesting, but it's all so small. Where are all those tall buildings that used to be here?* Even the reenactment of the gunfights seemed like something out of a questionably entertaining B movie.

Just about everything was—and is—pretty small in Dodge City, Kansas. As a boy, I saw the city and its legendary history through the eyes of a child. When I returned, nothing had changed except my perspective. What had once frightened me no longer had any power. I had put away my childish perspective and had begun to see Dodge City through adult eyes.

Your Ghost Towns

I hope you are making the relevant connections to your life. Are you keeping yourself from inner healing because you continue to look at past events or persons through the eyes of a child? What do you think would happen if you revisited some of the old ghost towns that haunt your memories? It would be a wonderful first step to removing the emotional pain that slows you down, keeps you burned out and exhausted, and prevents you from becoming the person God designed you to be.

To determine if memories of your past are controlling your present, ask yourself the following questions:

1. What negative memories seem to haunt me? Which events, and the pain they caused, are still vivid, as though they just happened?
2. What words or voices from the past are still ringing in my mind today?

If you find that past pain still has power over you today, you need to begin moving out of your past and into the present. Start moving out of the ghost town of the past by daily reminding yourself that those negative events are over and need no longer affect you. Think about the good things of the present and be thankful for them. Think about each of your abilities and gifts and how each has played a part in making you the unique person you are. You will have to make a daily decision to dismiss the hurtful memories of the past and concentrate on the positive things of today until the past no

---

We have been authorized by God to break free from our past with its tentacles that can squeeze the life out of us, making us fearful and weak.

---

longer controls your thoughts. The choice is yours. It will require some risk and demand a deeper trust of yourself—but that will only enhance your growth. In the end, all you will lose is your chains to the past. What you will gain is an opportunity to regain control of your life.

We all have the capacity to become what we were meant—authorized—to be. We have been authorized by God to break free from our past with its tentacles that can squeeze the life out of us, making us fearful and weak. Just as a graveyard is the most appropriate location for a resurrection, so can despair and exhaustion be the breeding grounds for hope. We can develop a vision for the future that believes an exciting, fulfilling life still lies ahead. It's a vision of hope and newness and a renewed perspective that the best is yet to come.

Shaped by Storms

In the beautiful city of Carmel, California, there is a famous, weathered and gnarled cypress tree growing out of solid rock on the edge of the beautiful and rugged California coast. The object of photographers worldwide, this tree is a growing symbol of tenacity and courage in the center of the ravages of nature. If that cypress could talk, it might complain about the coastal storms that have beat against its trunk and branches for so many years. It could lament the fierce winds and rain and curse those who have maliciously carved their initials on its weather-beaten trunk. But, wise tree that it is, the cypress would probably say, "I would not have the elegance I manifest today were it not for the pressure of the wind, rain, and storms throughout the years, because I have been shaped by their combined forces. I embraced them, and they embraced me. In the end, I remained vibrant and strong. I survived because I did not fight their seemingly unkind intrusions. Bruised? Yes, but I made the decision to grow my roots deeper into the rock, and I weathered the storm."

And so can you. The challenges of your life have shaped you up to this moment in your personal history. Some have been wrenching, terrible memories. Others were probably not as bad as you once thought. I just want to remind you that you did not always have control over what happened to you. In fact most of your early life experiences may have been completely out of your control. All the greater reason to view your earlier challenges from a fresh, new perspective and to see the past with adult eyes taking note of your struggles and past secrets in a light that will enhance your growth, give you hope for your better future, and bring inner healing.

Many times, however, past pain is so deep and embedded that we need to be willing to ask for help. If a person has been severely abused physically, psychologically, or sexually, that person must have help in dealing with the pain. The recovery from severe abuse requires the skilled knowledge of a professional counselor. Additional help may also be found in books written on the subject, such as *Haunted Memories* by Perry Draper (Revell, 1996), *Wounded Heart* by Dan Allender (NavPress, 1990), or my book *Healing the Scars of Emotional Abuse* (Revell, 1995).

To Forgive Is to Grow

In chapter 4 we talked about the importance of maintaining a forgiving spirit and this is especially important in overcoming the ghosts from our past. As long as we hold onto our resentments, we have no assurance of ever growing up. Instead, we will remain children—powerless, dependent, unable to separate ourselves from our parents, held in bondage to the past, with limited capacity to recover from emotional exhaustion.

That's why being able to forgive others for what they may have done to you is crucial to your emotional growth. Consider the process as *forgive and let go* and make the following credo part of your daily life.

To *forgive and let go* does not mean I stop caring; it does mean I will no longer take responsibility for the actions of others.

To *forgive and let go* is to admit powerlessness, which means the outcome is not in my hands.

To *forgive and let go* is not to try to change or blame another but to make the most of myself and recognize God's design for my life.

To *forgive and let go* is no longer to care for but to care about.

To *forgive and let go* is no longer to fix but to be aware.

To *forgive and let go* is no longer to judge but to allow another to be a human being.

To *forgive and let go* is no longer to be in the middle, arranging all the outcomes, but to allow others to choose their own destinies.

To *forgive and let go* is no longer to be protective but to permit others to create their own reality.

To *forgive and let go* is no longer to deny but to accept.

To *forgive and let go* is no longer to nag, scold, or argue but instead to search out my own shortcomings and correct them.

To *forgive and let go* is no longer to adjust everything to my desires but to take each day as it comes and cherish myself in God's plan for today.

To *forgive and let go* is no longer to criticize and regulate others but to try to become what I know God has created me to be.

To *forgive and let go* is no longer to regret the past but to grow and live for today and the future, using my past as material for growth.

Sam's Story

One person who had to learn to forgive and let go is a friend of mine named Sam. A son of a minister, Sam was a good boy as he grew up. Too good, perhaps. He minded his parents, was faithful in church, played in the fellowship band, led the singing in the services, and was well liked by all who met him.

As young Sam approached puberty, his interest in the church programs waned as he began to notice girls. One evening while watching television in his home, he made a remark to the effect of, That girl on TV is cute! His preacher father immediately grabbed young Sam by the scruff of the neck and escorted him unceremoniously into his private office where he locked the door and demanded that his young son drop his trousers. Sam was summarily whipped until the backs of both knees were red with huge welts—a beating that brought moanful cries from the boy. When the thrashing was finally over, his father, panting from his out-of-control rage, blew the dust off an encyclopedia of sex that was secreted behind a few books of systematic theology and missions and proceeded to shove graphic pictures of male and female genitalia in Sam's face.

"Okay, now you know what it's all about. This is your first lesson about sex. Now I never want to hear another word about it. Do you understand, son?"

"Yes, Father, I understand. I'm sorry," sobbed young Sam.

"Well then, I want you to know that I only whipped you because I love you and I want the best for you. You know that, Sam, don't you?"

"Yes, Father, I know you love me. I know that's why you hit me."

"Then let's pretend this whole thing never happened."

"Okay, Father. I promise I'll never mention it again."

And Sam didn't. Even though the whippings continued for many more years. Whippings for talking in church, whippings for talking back to his mother, whippings for wanting to

---

*To **forgive and let go** is no longer to criticize and regulate others but to try to become what I know God has created me to be.*

---

go to high school dances, whippings, whippings, whippings. Sam did not rebel, but the anger toward his father cut a deep swath across his soul. When Sam finally left home, he left for good. For years he could not forgive his father. His father's brutality had been confusing for a little boy and was equally confusing for Sam as a young man. Now it still confused him as an adult with children of his own.

Recently Sam went to see the film *Shine,* the story of a young pianist who endured much of the same kind of physical and emotional abuse Sam had received. During the movie, the remembrance of times past began to build imperceptibly in Sam's heart. The young man in the film was a child prodigy, a musical genius, but a lad whose dreams were daily shattered and abused by an excessively controlling father who had his own plans for his talented son. Sam sat in the darkened theater, the message creeping into his own consciousness, frame by frame. No popcorn and soda for Sam that night. Just blank stares at the screen, asking *why, why?*

Still, there was no immediate verbal reaction from Sam. But later as he and his wife drove home, it was as if an atomic bomb went off in Sam's soul. It started with the question he asked his wife: "Honey, why did my daddy do it to me? Why did he hit me so hard so long ago . . . and why does it still hurt so much today? Why? Why?"

Tears from Sam's reddened eyes fell in streams as waves of anger, pent up for more than forty-five years, burst forth like water spouting from an artesian well. Sam pulled into a deserted parking lot, got out of his car, and began striking the air in a rage that his frightened wife had never seen before. As his tears dropped to the already rain-soaked asphalt, Sam relived the pain of his youth as his chest heaved to the point of exhaustion. His voice went through so many levels and decibels, it was as if he was in the throes of an exorcism. Cursing his father for the beatings, he flailed at the wind, only to end up sobbing, face down on the trunk of his car where his tears and the rain became one.

Sam's rage continued as his wife drove him home. *Why? Why? And why was the rage so long in coming?* he asked. Never had Sam felt his pain so deeply. Never had he relived those moments of childhood with such passion. And when he had cried all he could cry, never was there a greater sense of cleansing and the beginning of forgiveness for what his father had done to him almost five decades earlier. Sam knew once the demons had been dealt with that it would be his turn to respond, and over the next few days he made a conscious decision to forgive his deceased father. He knew it was the only option that would lead to inner healing.

For many of us a willingness to forgive doesn't come as quickly as it did for Sam. It must be a process of relearning, or actually learning for the first time, how to love and then having the ability to forgive.

Sam learned, as we all must, that there is a kind of beauty in forgiveness. Not because we are able to erase past behavior that

---

Forgiveness sees and feels the wound but goes beyond the physical and mental pain to demonstrate a willingness to start over without opening the door to further abuse of any kind.

---

has hurt us. We do not eliminate the past events by trying to *think* them away—that's denial. Forgiveness, instead, is when, in the midst of remembering the pain, we learn to open our hearts and accept the one who did us harm and welcome that person with wholehearted acceptance. Forgiveness sees and feels the wound but goes beyond the physical and mental pain to demonstrate a willingness to start over without opening the door to further abuse of any kind.

Author Jim Smoke has said that forgiveness is:

a decision, not a feeling
showing mercy even when the injury has been deliberate
accepting the person as he or she is
taking a risk; making yourself vulnerable

accepting an apology

choosing to love

Whom do you need to forgive? What words do you need to say, either quietly in your heart, in a letter you never deliver, or face to face? I don't need to give you a script. You will know what to say when the time comes to say it, and when it is said, yet another ghost will be exorcised from your past, and you will regain control of your life. If you have difficulty doing this on your own, seek the help of a professional counselor or therapist.

A Prayer for Kindness

There's something else that is important in our quest for strength and courage, and that's a spirit of kindness. Too often we teach our children the verse, "Be kind one to another" (Eph. 4:32 RSV), and then we forget the admonition as adults. True forgiveness and kindness are cut from the same cloth; it is impossible to demonstrate one without declaring the other.

I find it interesting that the word *kind* comes from the Old English *cynd* for kin or family—a place where kindness is too often in such short supply. It's within the home where we first learn to recognize important familial boundaries, and where we develop a deep respect for others. Yet how especially difficult it is to embrace those people associated with ghostly encounters from our past.

If it is difficult for you to be kind to those who have hurt you, consider praying this prayer that has helped me on so many occasions:

Keep me, O God, from pettiness; let me be large in thought, in word, in deed. As I look into my past with its pain and fear, may I see my hurt through eyes of love. Let me be done with faultfinding and leave off self-seeking. May I put away all pretense and meet others face to face—without self-pity and without prejudice. May I never be hasty in my judgment, but generous. Let me take time for all things; make me grow calm, serene, gentle. You did not create me to be burned out and exhausted but to be an effective person who does your bidding. Teach me to put into action my better impulses, straightforward and unafraid. Grant that I may realize that it is the little things that create differences, that in the big things of life we are as one. And, O Lord God, help me to recognize that if I would be strong again, I must remember always to be loving and kind. Amen.

Growing through the Storms

Your road to becoming strong again must work through the whole series of past storms that have wreaked havoc on your body, soul, and spirit. But the good news is that now you know you weathered those storms; they helped you grow in ways that you were not even aware and they have shaped you

---

*Often it's only when our eyes have been washed clear
with buckets of tears that we will ever get a handle on the
larger vision for ourselves and our place in the world.*

---

into the person you have now become. Often it's only when our eyes have been washed clear with buckets of tears that we will ever get a handle on the larger vision for ourselves and our place in the world. Although you may never fully understand why or how the storms of your past have freshened the air you breathe today, you can find a healthy, new perspective that grants you the freedom to:

Take time to think; it is the source of your power.

Take time to play; it is the secret of your youth.

Take time to read; it is the foundation of your knowledge.

Take time to dream; it will take you to the stars.

Take time to laugh; it really is your best medicine.

Take time to pray; it is your touch with almighty God.

Take time to reach out to others; it will give your life significance.

Make your life prime time, and be ready to expect God to give you a hundredfold return as you exorcise the ghosts from your past and see old challenges with adult eyes as you take one step closer to becoming strong again.

Reflect, Renew, Rebuild

Reflect. It's hard to believe that a person like Mother Teresa ever fell victim in anger or animosity to her past. Perhaps it's because of how she always saw the impoverished of body and spirit through the eyes of Christ. As you ponder those difficult areas of your past—ghosts that may still haunt you and that remain hurtful—allow the words Mother Teresa often spoke to sweep over your spirit: "I come to you, Jesus, to take your touch before I begin my day. Let your eyes rest upon my eyes for awhile. Let me take to my work the assurance of your friendship. Fill my mind to the last, through the desert of noise. Let your blessed sunshine fill my thoughts, and give me strength for those who need me."

Renew. Write out the following eight affirmations and carry these powerful messages with you in your purse or wallet.

Review them at least three times each day for thirty days. This is the time necessary to either break or create a new habit. These affirmations will be your daily reminder of the progress you are making as you exorcise the ghosts of your past.

1. Because I'm dealing with my past, I am enjoying the freedom to feel great about myself today.
2. Because I'm dealing with my past, I am enjoying the freedom to have healthy relationships.
3. Because I'm dealing with my past, I have the freedom to live at peace with God.
4. Because I'm dealing with my past, I am giving myself the freedom to enjoy vibrant health.
5. Because I'm dealing with my past, I am free to live apart from others' abuse.
6. Because I'm dealing with my past, I am giving myself the freedom to have fun as never before.
7. Because I'm dealing with my past, I have the freedom to be a healthy giver because I have adopted an attitude of gratitude.
8. Because I'm dealing with my past, I can now echo the words of the promise from God's Word, "You will know the truth, and the truth will set you free" (John 8:32).

Rebuild. If there is a person—living or dead—who continues to be a ghost in your past, I invite you to take time to write that person a letter that comes straight from your heart. Be honest with your feelings, and then communicate that you forgive what he or she did to you, that you no longer hold grudges, and that you are moving on in a spirit of forgiveness. Then, destroy the letter. You will have done all the work necessary to bring you one step closer to becoming strong again.

6

Self-Care

Eight Secrets for Finding All the Energy You'll Ever Need

The world is sown with good: but unless I turn my glad thoughts into practical living and till my own field, I cannot reap a kernel of the good.

Helen Keller

As you were growing up, your parents may have been a great source of strength for you. They went to your soccer games, your dances, your school plays. They sat on the front row applauding so loudly that you were embarrassed with this unashamed demonstration of parental pride. If this has been your experience, you are among the very fortunate. I'm sure you'd connect with the grateful words of Ulysses S. Grant: "I was successful because you believed in me." You felt cared for, respected, honored, loved.

On the other hand, you may not have had this kind of parent-child relationship. Your father or mother may have been aloof, cold, seemingly uncaring—even abusive. You may have gone to your games and dances alone, performed

---

"I was successful because you believed in me."
Ulysses S. Grant

---

alone, came home alone, and cried your eyes out night after night because you felt your parents didn't care or understand or were too busy working to notice you. If that has been your past, I feel deeply for you, because it has made part of your life more difficult. It may have even built in a kind of weakness that is still giving you fits.

Lucy was angry when she came to see me. She was a grown woman, mother of three, successful in her profession, but still so very angry at her father for not coming to her basketball games and school plays when she was in junior high. And I mean she was enraged. In tears she told me, "Dr. Jantz, why didn't he come to my games and performances? I'd look up in the stands or squint out into the darkened hall, hoping against hope that he'd be there, but he never was. When I'd ask him why, he'd always promise that he'd come to the next event or the next. But he never did. And now here I am, thirty-five years old, still waking up nights crying and wondering why he didn't care enough to want to be with me during those important times in my life. Now he's gone, and I'll never have the father I always wanted."

We all need someone to yell, "Attaboy, attagirl," from the sidelines of life. Sometimes this special person shows up; sometimes he or she does not. Either way, we need to understand *that's the way it was*. We must play the cards as they are dealt if we are to have any chance to become strong again. We have the opportunity to make some decisions that could dramatically improve our emotional and physical health. We have the capacity to design a life filled with hope, strength, and joy. Edmund Spenser wrote, "It is the mind that maketh good or ill, that maketh wretched or happy, rich or poor."

We once depended on others for our strength and our self-esteem. At one time they were all we had to count on—for good or for ill. But now we're adults—on our own. No longer must we lean on others to care for us. Rather, we need to learn these eight secrets of self-care to help us find all the energy we need for living.

Each of these secrets was born out of my own bout with emotional exhaustion several years ago. I hope it takes you less time to put these secrets into practice than it took me. One thing I promise: These secrets will work for you if you are willing to practice them.

Secret 1—Create Small Pleasures

I'd like you to answer these two questions:

1. What small pleasures do you truly enjoy more than anything else?
2. How long has it been since you've engaged in these pleasures?

I wish I could hear your answers, because if you feel stressed and burned out to the point of emotional exhaustion, there's a good chance you no longer enjoy the little things that used to make you happy.

Think back to an earlier time before the pressures of life began to encroach on your spirit. Did you ever enjoy camping, hiking in the great outdoors and making a fire for that first cup of black coffee on a cold, frosty morning? Perhaps you once enjoyed the theater or band concerts in the park. Did you support the local high school football team as they battled it out with their cross-town rivals on Friday nights? You may have once taken the time to wash and wax your car, taking pride in how the shiny hood reflected your smiling face as you'd give it one more swish of the cloth. *Small pleasures.*

You may have once been a regular volunteer at your local rescue mission, helping to feed the poor. You may have read to the elderly or helped a child and her parents from another country learn English. Perhaps you used to visit a convalescent home during the holidays to bring cheer to those who had no family or friends. *Small pleasures.*

Or it may have been something as simple as riding a bicycle, chopping wood and enjoying a roaring fire, walking each morning with a friend, or taking a minivacation to enjoy the pristine beauty of the world your heavenly Father has created. Perhaps you once spent hours each weekend in your garden, planting seeds, fertilizing, and watching it grow. You may even have once been a grower of prizewinning roses. *Small pleasures.*

I hope I've captured the essence of some of the small pleasures of your past. If I haven't, please take the liberty to fill in the blanks. Recognizing your small pleasures is important because it's doing the little, seemingly unimportant things that bring the deep richness to our lives. They renew us, refresh us, and help us see beyond ourselves.

It's not the next big financial deal that brings us renewal. It's not grinding along for another two hours on the freeway that contributes to our solace and peace. Responsible people do what they must do, of course. But one of the secrets of finding inner healing is to know how to slow down, change our routines, make room for small pleasures, smell the roses, and not take ourselves too seriously. If we fail to do this, we will keep focusing inward, which will ultimately isolate us from others and prevent us from seeing God's goodness all around us.

When you begin to slow down, relax, and reengage in small pleasures, you'll feel like the psalmist who wrote, "I will

---

It's doing the little, seemingly unimportant things that bring the deep richness to our lives. They renew us, refresh us, and help us see beyond ourselves.

---

lift mine eyes unto the hills, from whence cometh my help" (Ps. 121:1 KJV). We will never see the hills if we're looking at ourselves, and our hearts will never be elevated if we fail to lift our eyes. As we engage in small pleasures, we lift up our eyes. What small pleasures can you enjoy today to help you rebuild your sense of balance?

Secret 2—Make Exercise Fun

In a recent seminar I gave on one of my books, *Losing Weight Permanently: Secrets of the 2% Who Succeed*,[1] I asked the audience to tell me what the word *exercise* meant to them. For the next thirty seconds I heard about everything:

"I hate it."

"No fun."

"I have no time."

"Exercise is work."

"Not for me."

"I know I should, but it's just a pain."

"I can't lose weight anyway, so why try?"

"I joined two fitness clubs, and that didn't work."

One wealthy man joked, "I hire other people to work out for me." Noting his girth, I wasn't so sure he was kidding!

My friend Covert Bailey, in his delightful book *The New Fit or Fat*, brings more fun and frolic to the subject of fitness than anyone I know. I love it when he says,

> Start so slowly that people make fun of you. . . . Gentle exercise pays off. If you are exercising at a slow pace, one that is only 65 percent of your maximum heart rate, your body will adapt and profit from the exercise. You may just be walking and it may not seem like much to you and your friends, but at night as you sleep, your body will say, "Boy, she doesn't exercise very hard, but she sure does a lot of it. I better adapt to it."[2]

Covert's right, of course. And while you are "starting so slowly that people make fun of you," do it with a friend. Not one who is too fit though—that might discourage you from ever exercising again. Instead, start walking, hiking, or biking with someone who's not out to shatter an Olympic record. Make your exercise fun but at the same time don't stop at every other house to chat with a neighbor and have a cup of coffee. Maintain a gentle but steady pace as you talk with your friend or listen to your Walkman, smell the flowers, and enjoy some scenery you may not have noticed for years.

This secret is important because you really do need to engage in some form of exercise several times a week to help you move away from your mental and physical exhaustion and toward emotional freedom. You don't need to be afraid of the *E* word. *Exercise* is not doing aerobics like those trim young gals in bikinis on late-night infomercials, nor is it pumping iron like the well-greased, muscular men and women who show us more body than we're actually interested in seeing. Exercise is not just running marathons, extreme skiing, two-hundred-mile cycling events, or spending hours a week at the fitness center. Exercise can be as simple as a ten-minute walk each day with a friend, riding a bike at your own pace, or playing tennis. Before you know it, you'll be doing your activity for twenty or thirty minutes, perhaps even an hour every day. If you make it fun, you won't even look at your watch.

Remember, you do not need a sauna suit, one-hundred-dollar walking shoes, expensive exercise equipment, coordinated workout clothes, a gym membership, a trampoline, or an abdominal machine. These paraphernalia give exercise a bad name. You don't need them. The Nike Corporation has given us a great slogan: "Just Do It!" Don't wait another minute. Until now you may have been too busy to exercise because you thought exercise had to be drudgery. Here's the good news: You *can* slow down and enjoy the flowers. You don't have to control everything in your life. That's probably what got you in trouble in the first place. Making exercise fun will help put you into an environment that's free and easy. Your stress will slowly melt away, and you will find yourself one step closer to regaining control of your life.

What exercise could you begin today? Could you persuade a friend to enjoy it with you? If you're ever in Edmonds,

---

Exercise can be as simple as a ten-minute walk each day with a friend, riding a bike at your own pace, or playing tennis.

Washington, go for a walk and enjoy the beauty of Puget Sound, snow-capped mountain ranges, and eagles flying overhead, perhaps ending your walk with a hot latte at a local coffeehouse. I'm sure you have lovely places to walk in your hometown. Enjoy the beauty and come to realize that living life faster is not necessarily better.

Secret 3—Develop Three Relationships of Significance

Faced with mounting pressures from all sides, it's no wonder that 68 percent of executives see burnout as a serious problem, and nearly half think depression is on the rise among their peers. Sixty-five percent believe their peers work too many hours, 64 percent are physically exhausted by the end of the day, 60 percent often bring too much work home, and 58 percent say emotional exhaustion is common. And it's not only business executives who are victims of burnout. Emotional exhaustion is becoming epidemic among all members of society.

Today Melissa came into my office to talk about her life that's fast becoming unraveled: troubled with insomnia, plagued with a recurrent weight problem, and stressed to the point that she had even considered taking her own life. Melissa, a critical care nurse, had been on call twenty-four hours a day for several days. For months, her life had not been her own. She had given everything for her career, and now it was taking its toll.

As we talked together, I realized Melissa really had no friends. She had acquaintances, colleagues, and people with whom she'd have coffee at the hospital—but she had no soul mates. I suggested to Melissa that a spirited, renewed vitality could come about by nurturing three kinds of friendships:

1. A relationship with someone older and wiser, who'd lived long enough to understand the value of trusting, intimate friendships. This would be someone Melissa could just enjoy, listen to, and learn from without needing to make a major contribution.
2. Seek to build a friendship with someone her own age—a person she could easily relate to because of

shared interests and values, a true peer. Immediately Melissa thought of a woman at her church she would like to get to know better but with whom she had hardly ever spoken.

3. Find some time each month to be a mentor to a person younger than she. Melissa said that because she is bilingual, she might like to help a foreign-born child in the inner city with his or her English.

At first I was afraid Melissa was almost too eager to establish these relationships. But the more we talked about developing friendships that were important and meaningful to her, the more relaxed she became about reaching out and extending herself to others. Rather than these relationships becoming a drain on her already overscheduled life, she began to look for holes in her schedule so she could get off her treadmill of frustration and fatigue and start touching the lives of others. Melissa started seeing these three potential relationships as an exquisite mixed bouquet, each flower making its unique contribution to the beauty and fragrance of the whole. She made the commitment to go beyond herself and to learn again how to be a friend.

Will you consider taking seriously this secret of establishing at least three relationships of significance as you seek inner healing? Could you start today?

Secret 4—Live with an Attitude of Gratitude

In the early days of the settlement of the wild West, the pioneers encountered tremendous obstacles. It was day after day of physical and emotional deprivation. Some made it; many did not, and the trails were littered with tiny crosses of the brave but dead. One party of pioneers on the Oregon Trail had suffered for weeks from a scarcity of water and grass for their animals. Most of their wagons had broken down, causing endless delays in the stifling heat. Along with these adverse circumstances came a general feeling of fretfulness and futility. Optimism and cheer were gone. Courage was in limited supply.

One night the leaders called a special meeting for the express purpose of airing complaints. When they had gathered around the campfire, one of the pioneers stood up and said, "Before we commence with our grief session—the reason for this assembly tonight—don't you think we should at least first thank God that he has brought us this far with no loss of life, with no serious trouble from the Indians, and that we have enough strength left to finish our journey?" The other settlers agreed, and after the brief prayer, all that could be

---

Finding God-given blessing in every hour of distress is one of the most important keys to bouncing back, being resilient, and becoming strong again.

---

heard were the lone cries of a pack of wolves in the distance. There was otherwise stone silence around the campfire, because no one had any grievances they felt were important enough to voice.

They suddenly realized if they couldn't be satisfied with what they'd received, they could at least be thankful for what they had escaped. In that moment their thankfulness transformed a grumbling spirit into one of contentment, enabling them to see the many mercies of God that they had been overlooking.

Finding God-given blessing in every hour of distress is one of the most important keys to bouncing back, being resilient, and becoming strong again. On the other hand, a spirit of ingratitude is like having rickets of the mind. It's a disease that produces disappointment, conflict, animosity, fear, and self-centeredness. I can't think of anything good about being ungrateful. We need to learn that a high AQ (attitude quotient) is going to make us happier, help us enjoy life more, and create a greater assortment of good friends than a high IQ.

You and I will never be without trouble. Job 5:7 says, "Yet man is born to trouble as surely as sparks fly upward." We can do little about that. However, we don't have to focus on and be consumed by our troubles.

In his moving book *Now That I Have Cancer, I Am Whole*, John Robert McFarland provides an enormous insight into thanks-based living: "I'm so grateful I never have bad days. I have nauseated days and frightened days. Tired days and hurting days. Long days and short days. Silent days and alone days. Mouth-sore days and swollen-hand days. Bald days and diarrhea days. Rainy days and sunny days. Cold days and warm days. But no bad days. I'm so grateful."[3]

Could you be grateful under those circumstances? Could I? Would our hurt, disappointment, and pain overshadow what is still good—life itself? What are you most grateful for? What blessing have you been taking for granted? Are you willing to be grateful for it now in a fresh, new way? Can you open your heart with the apostle Paul, who wrote:

Encourage the fainthearted, help the weak, be patient with them all. See that none of you repays evil for evil, but always seek to do good to one another and to all. Rejoice always, pray constantly, give thanks in all circumstances; for this is the will of God in Christ Jesus for you.

1 Thessalonians 5:14–18 RSV

Secret 5—Practice Becoming a Life-Giving Person

As Mahatma Gandhi stepped aboard a train one day, one of his shoes slipped from his foot and landed on the track. The train was already pulling away from the station, and he was unable to retrieve his shoe. To the astonishment of his traveling companions, Gandhi calmly took off his other shoe and threw it back along the track to land close to the one he'd dropped. "Why did you do that?" asked an amazed fellow passenger. Gandhi smiled, "The poor man who finds that shoe lying near the track will now have a pair he can use."

Gandhi did that sort of thing instinctively. His decisions were life-giving, and they had a ripple effect wherever he went, so much so that an entrenched British colonial empire was brought to its knees through his acts of nonviolence. As a man, Gandhi appeared to be so physically weak that it seemed a small breeze might knock him over. Yet he was so very strong, resilient, and integrity tough. Why? Because he knew the difference between giving and taking away.

I'm sure you know individuals from both camps. Think for a moment of the people whose company you enjoy and cherish. Are they not men and women who are life-giving?

Think for a moment of the people whose company you enjoy and cherish. Are they not men and women who are life-giving?

They are interested in you, they listen to you, they regard you as their friend, and their smile is a tonic. Then there are the takers—those who brighten up a room when they leave because they have chipped away at your self-esteem and left you weather-beaten.

Ralph Waldo Emerson wrote, "The only gift is a portion of thyself." In my counseling sessions I see that many of us think we are giving up part of ourselves when we give of ourselves.

In fact, the opposite is true. One of the most effective antidotes for burnout and emotional exhaustion is to become a life-giving person and to stop demanding, threatening, pleading, cajoling, and bribing others to do our bidding. To gain inner healing, we must understand that loving attention paid to other people's goals and dreams is the greatest form of compassion and caring.

We have a wonderful example to follow in the One who said:

> I am the Good Shepherd. The Good Shepherd lays down his life for the sheep (John 10:11 TLB).

> I have come as a Light to shine in this dark world, so that all who put their trust in me will no longer wander in the darkness (John 12:46 TLB).

> I am the Gate. Those who come in by way of the Gate will be saved and will go in and out and find green pastures (John 10:9 TLB).

A Shepherd, a Light, and a Gate: the laying down of a life, a light shining in the darkness, a way in and a way out. Our heavenly Father provides us with the necessary ingredients you and I need to help harness our fears, banish our exhaustion, and put us on the road to emotional health. What can you do today, with Christ's help, to show someone how much you care? It doesn't need to be a major event, because it's still the little things that mean the most.

Secret 6—Allow Food to Nourish You Again

You really are what you eat! Consider this information from the U.S. Department of Agriculture:

- In 1994, the average American consumed twenty-two pounds of salty snacks such as pretzels, potato chips, popcorn, and cheese puffs—a four-pound increase over 1988. The average amount spent per person on these munchies was $57.10.
- The five most common orders in restaurants in 1994 were carbonated beverages, french fries, hamburgers, pizzas, and side salads.
- The average American consumes nearly thirty pounds of hamburger per year.
- About a third of all vegetables Americans eat are white potatoes.

This is not happy news, and because it is a distressing report, I'm going to give a bit more space to this issue of learning how to let food nourish you again. While the statistics may have improved slightly in the last few years, most North Americans still continue to forget that the purpose of food is to nourish their bodies. Those who have succumbed to emotional exhaustion have an even greater need for proper nourishment. Their emotional stress often has a physical impact, not allowing the nutrients of good food to do their necessary work.

It was because of this epidemic of poor food management I observed in so many of my clients that I decided to write the book *Losing Weight Permanently: Secrets of the 2% Who Succeed.* I'd like to share with you a few passages from this book because it is so vital for you to understand the part that nourishing food plays in your becoming strong again.

Sally was overweight, unhappy, and on the brink of emotional exhaustion. After numerous counseling sessions, this is what she decided to do:

One . . . I started eating a simple, healthy breakfast each morning. That was my only guideline . . . that it had to be healthy. No list of special foods, no restrictive diet, no calories to count, lie about or eat. Nothing. What surprised me was that I was being asked to make my *own* decisions, and not rely on someone else's idea of what I should consume. I was given complete freedom to eat when I wanted, and how much I wanted. It just had to be healthy. Actually, this frightened me, because I wanted to be told what to do.[4]

Sally really was frightened when I asked her to make her own decisions about food and about making food the right kind of friend. Here's the rest of Sally's story:

So I chose to eat a large breakfast of whole grain cereal and lowfat milk and some fruit each morning. It was bulky so it made me feel full. It wasn't sugary, so my insulin level did not increase. I knew all about this theoretically, but it wasn't easy to put into practice. A big part of me (which was most of me) hated it. At first I missed my usual two jelly donuts and three cups of coffee with lots of cream, followed in a few minutes by grazing in the fridge for a few leftovers from the night before. But I'd made an agreement with Dr. Jantz to do this, and besides I was desperate.

The second thing was even more amazing to me. I was asked not to weigh myself at *all* in between sessions. I'd already sent my scale "on vacation," so there was no way to weigh myself at home. But I was not to weigh myself *anywhere*. This was difficult. How would I know if I was making any progress if I couldn't weigh myself two or three times a day as I'd done most of my life? I didn't understand it, but I said I'd stick with the program and obey the rules.[5]

I'm happy to report that Sally is doing quite well, self-correcting along the way as she's still tempted to return to her old way of thinking about food. She's rediscovering what food is all about—it's there to nourish her body and is not a substance for abuse.

When recovering from emotional exhaustion, you quickly learn the benefits of decreasing the amount of fat and refined carbohydrates in your diet. Some of us grew up with mothers who loved to prepare big, fattening sack lunches for us to eat at school. The sandwiches were works of art, prepared on soft slices of enriched white bread, overlaid with greasy salami, bologna, and thick layers of mayonnaise and butter. Nestled in the bottom of the bag would be a love note accompanied by two or three large, freshly baked chocolate or peanut butter cookies. Our mothers may have had the best of intentions for us, but those good wishes later may have brought on disaster as we struggled with our weight, which contributed to our mounting stress.

When you start to take seriously the reports of the increased risk of heart disease and cancer associated with these high levels of fat, I hope you will quickly choose to self-correct. You will read food labels more carefully and seek to interpret the wealth of information they contain. This is a far cry from the ineffective calorie counting and roller-coaster dieting you may have engaged in before. You will also stop frying your foods and breading your meats. You will learn that broiling, baking, and even microwave preparation are better alternatives to cooking foods in fats and oil. You will also begin to investigate food supplements that are specifically designed to help rebalance the body chemistry of those who are emotionally and physically exhausted. I've included information in the appendix on vitamin supplements and suggestions for healthy eating.

Sally had to learn that dieting and bingeing were terrible obstacles to her stressed physical health and mental stability.

Each round of dieting caused increased hypertension and a rise in her blood pressure. When she finally understood that dieting and bingeing were making her more prone to stress-related illnesses, heart and kidney disease, and stroke, she knew she had to make a change. To do this, Sally had to start listening to her body. She had actually forgotten what it was like to eat normally. In the past, she had engaged in so much secret eating, squirreling away money for snacks, and hoarding of food that she no longer knew what it was like to eat food to provide nourishment and strength for her body.

That's why Sally had to learn the art of eating regularly again—three times a day. Unlike the earlier breakfasts of fattening bakery items, her breakfasts now satisfy her until noon, when she can eat a good lunch without even thinking about bingeing. And it all started with a commitment to a proven, effective program of permanent weight loss and a deep desire to join the 2 percent who succeed in losing weight permanently.

Can you relate to Sally? Perhaps now is the time that you, too, need to learn to see food as healing you, making you strong, and filling you with vitality. You can begin by making the following commitment.

I hate fat enough to:

Take action right now, because I know it is contributing to my stress and emotional exhaustion.

Throw out the bags of snack foods I've hidden in the cupboard, even though I paid good money to buy them.

Eat an apple or orange before I go to the movies so I'm not tempted to buy junk food. (And I won't eat popcorn just because it's a movie!)

Begin treating myself as a person created in God's image and, therefore, believe I am someone definitely worth caring for.

Signed _____

Date _____

Secret 7—Develop Your Sense of Humor

Much of what we fret and strain about can be handled in more creative ways. Proverbs 17:22 says, "A cheerful heart is good medicine." While emotional exhaustion and especially past abuse in any form is no laughing matter, I invite you to look back and find specific circumstances at which you can now honestly laugh. Humor is one of the most effective stress busters around.

A good belly laugh at the comedy routines of the Three Stooges, Abbot and Costello, or Laurel and Hardy relaxes muscles, reduces blood pressure, and may even lower levels of hormones that produce stress and suppress your immunity to illness. According to William F. Fry, a psychiatrist associated with Stanford University, laughter stimulates the production of hormones called catecholamines, which are believed to release endorphins—the same stress reducers triggered by vigorous exercise.

Although it is getting harder to find good, clean humor in modern comedy shows, it is there if you look. For example, one of God's greatest gifts to us today is Charlie "Tremendous" Jones—a delightful, energetic, disarming communicator. If you've never heard Charlie, do yourself a favor and find out where he's speaking next and go experience this man's humor. If you haven't really laughed for a while, buy his book *Humor Is Tremendous*.[6] You'll laugh yourself silly.

I like what Joel Goodman, the director of *The Humor Project*, says when he recommends imagining how our favorite comedians would react to the same situation. He suggests we try asking

---

A good belly laugh at the comedy routines of the Three Stooges, Abbot and Costello, or Laurel and Hardy relaxes muscles, reduces blood pressure, and may even lower levels of hormones that produce stress and suppress your immunity to illness.

---

ourselves what people like Lily Tomlin or Jerry Seinfeld might say if they were in our shoes. What a great idea! Let's look for humorous spins to some former frustration, anger, or pain. And by the way, smiling—even when you don't feel like it—helps too. Research now has proven that your facial expressions—smiles or frowns—actually can change your mood.

Secret 8—Ask God to Increase Your Faith

Author Jack Canfield tells a great story about what he experienced while driving home from work one day. He stopped to watch a local Little League baseball game that was being played in a park near his home. As Jack sat down behind the bench on the first baseline, he asked one of the boys what the score was.

"We're behind fourteen to nothing," the lad answered with a smile.

"Really," Jack responded, "I have to say you don't look very discouraged."

"Discouraged?" the boy asked, puzzled. "Why should we be discouraged? We haven't been up to bat yet."

What a wonderful message for those of us who have done battle with the scourge of emotional exhaustion. Sometimes we worry too much about what the opposing pitcher is going to throw at us when we haven't even had our turn at bat. Perhaps we've struck out so often that our courage and confidence is gone forever. Don't let past failures rob you of faith in future possibilities.

When I was so emotionally exhausted that I didn't know up from down, reality from fantasy, truth from fiction, it was only as I asked God to increase my faith, help my unbelief, and show me that he really had a plan designed for me that my life began to turn around. I had to finally admit I had a problem, swallow my pride, confess I didn't know it all, and

---

Of all the secrets we have worked through in this chapter, I'm confident that this is the one that will turn the tide for you as well: learning to ask God to increase your faith.

---

break down, crying out to the God of my salvation. Of all the secrets we have worked through in this chapter, I'm confident that this is the one that will turn the tide for you as well: learning to ask God to increase your faith. When God increases your faith, you will find many positive changes:

Faith looks for the good in yourself and others instead of harping on the worst.

Faith opens doors where despair slams them shut.

Faith discovers what can be done instead of grumbling about what cannot.

Faith draws its power from a deep trust in our heavenly Father and from an awareness that while we as human beings are not all good, neither are we all bad.

Faith creates flashes of light instead of cursing the darkness.

Faith regards problems, small and large, as opportunities.

Faith cherishes no illusions, nor does it yield to the temptation of cynicism.

Faith sets big goals and is not frustrated by repeated challenges or setbacks.

Faith pushes ahead when it would be easy to quit.

Faith puts up with modest gains, realizing that the longest journey begins with a single, often faltering step.

Faith accepts misunderstandings and even confusion as the price for serving the greater good of others.

Faith is a good loser because it has the divine assurance of victory.

It is my prayer that you will ask God to increase your faith and help you see his bigger, better plan for you—a plan that has no room for burnout or emotional exhaustion but instead one that promises a life of balance, courage, and love for yourself, for others, and for your heavenly Father. As your faith increases, you can claim as your motto this verse of ultimate encouragement: "In the world you have tribulation; but be of good cheer, I have overcome the world" (John 16:33 RSV). Once you and I knew very little of God's mercy and kindness. Now we are allowing his love and mercy to sweep over us and to make us strong again.

—— *Reflect, Renew, Rebuild* ——

Reflect. I encourage you to put the contents of this chapter to the test for the next thirty days. Then write me a postcard or letter, telling me how these secrets have impacted your life. (The Center's address, fax, and email are located at the back of the book.) When I receive your note, I will send you a specially recorded cassette tape to help you continue to grow as you recover from emotional exhaustion.

Renew. Take out your journal and list three simple pleasures you plan to start enjoying during the next ten days (secret 1). Write the reasons you have chosen these three pleasures and what you expect to receive from doing them. Go through the remaining secrets and note in your journal how you plan to implement each one. Then put them into practice.

Rebuild. To increase your faith, choose at least one psalm to read each week. Read it carefully and slowly and as often as possible. Then write in your journal any personal applications that may come to mind. If possible, use the translation *The Message*—one of the most easily understood versions available today.[7] I suggest you begin with Psalm 139.

7

Six Disciplines for Eliminating Self-Defeating Attitudes

Life does not consist—mainly or even largely—of facts and happenings. It consists mainly of the storm of thoughts that are forever blowing through one's mind.

Mark Twain

During the darkest days of World War II, when the Allies were struggling and losing on every front, Winston Churchill had the uncanny capacity to quiet his active mind by focusing on some entirely new—often offbeat—activity and giving it his undivided attention. Later, he could return to the strategies of meeting head-on the hated German war machine with his keen mind rested and refreshed.

I can't think of many people in the history of the world who have held more responsibility in their hands or had more monstrous crises to face than Winston Churchill during the years when he was prime minister of England. However, not everyone realizes he was able to face up to the sort of challenges that would have killed a dozen lesser individuals because of a pattern of behavior he had developed early on—a system for eliminating self-defeating attitudes. Fortunately Churchill's system is bound by neither time nor geography and can operate as freely and effectively in the wars you and I fight in our minds today.

The Master Key

In the context of learning to change gears while in the center of mental conflict, I once heard commentator Earl Nightingale read a quote by Winston Churchill that explained how the great statesman could concentrate on the many affairs of government without becoming stressed. He would consciously force himself to think about things that were completely unrelated to the problems before him.

Winston Churchill knew how to tap into one of the primary antidotes for emotional exhaustion: Change your focus momentarily so you can come back to face your challenges with fresh insights. Without using the exact words, Churchill was sharing with us one of the keys to regaining control of our lives.

We all know how a negative life view can keep us trapped, fearful, and stuck with choices that ruin any opportunity we might have for success. Let's look at six proven, practical disciplines that, when implemented, can turn an attitude of defeat and despair into hope, energy, and confidence.

Discipline 1—All Attitudes Must Be Reviewed and Renewed Daily

Notre Dame football coach Lou Holtz would tell his players, "Ability is what you're capable of doing. Motivation determines what you do. Attitude determines how well you do it." Victor Frankl, survivor of a Nazi prison camp and beacon of light for hundreds of other prisoners suffering under Hitler's Third Reich wrote, "The last of the human freedoms is to choose one's attitude in any given set of circumstances."

Isn't it amazing that a football coach and a prisoner of war are saying the same thing—that it's not our circumstances that hold us back but rather the attitudes we display *in* our circumstances? We all know people who delight in laughing at the cockeyed optimist—the one who always seems to be happy and on top of things, the person who has a bumper sticker on her car that declares, "Business is great, the sky is blue, and people are wonderful." But what's wrong with this?

A life of cynical pessimism is a poor second choice and does nothing but drive us deeper into sadness and depression, making us weaker, not stronger, and ultimately setting us up for emotional exhaustion. Oscar Wilde said a pessimist is one who, when confronted with the choice of two evils, chooses both. Bad way to live.

On the other hand, a spirit of optimism is life-giving. People who are upbeat regardless of their physical or emotional circumstances look for the good, just as bees gravitate to the center of a flower for their honey-making resource. But it's not a onetime flyby. The bees in your garden need to fly back to gather the pollen from the flower again and again, even as the best of attitudes must be constantly refreshed through daily action. It's the only way we can keep them positive, vibrant, and alive.

Since we know the reviewing and renewing of our attitudes begins with the renewing of our minds, we can see why the apostle Paul found it necessary to write:

But now you must rid yourselves of all such things as these: anger, rage, malice, slander, and filthy language from your lips. Do not lie to each other, since you have taken off your old self with its practices and have put on the new self, which is being *renewed* in knowledge in the image of its Creator.

Colossians 3:8–10 (italics added)

Without a regular renewal of our attitudes, we will remain stagnant and uninteresting, and will be able to offer little to those who need us most. It's just not possible to win at life and relationships with a self-defeating, unrenewed, boring, business-as-usual attitude. That's why the real attitude winners are the ones who:

Provide valuable service to others before thinking of their own needs

When discouraged, dig deep to the source of their faith and confidence

When trapped in a tunnel of misfortune, believe there will be light at the end of the tunnel

When roadblocked by poor decisions, remember that God is still in control and that no failure is ever final

Know that the greatest degrees one can earn are not academic but degrees of growth, persistence, and compassion for others

Discipline 2—Get Physical

Some of my best ideas and most profound attitude adjustments come while I'm cycling or jogging. While jogging I can actually run the gamut from thinking negatively about a problem, to being open to new possibilities, to actually coming up with a positive solution to my concerns—all during a few miles of physical exertion. Perhaps you've had the same experience. Brisk walking, running, cycling, hiking—any kind of physical exercise that's challenging for you—can help you see your life's problems with new eyes and can, in fact, even alter your attitude. Let me give you an example:

The other day while training for a half-marathon, I was thinking about some of the challenges we were facing at The Center, where we provide a nurturing environment for adults and children to talk about their lives. I love my work, and the rewards far outdistance the difficulties. But as with any business, not all aspects of it are pleasant. As I started my run this particular day, I was pretty much down on a couple people—and on myself for my reaction to some of the things they had said.

The first couple of miles I heaped one negative thought on another. I was making mental mincemeat of those people, thinking, *Just who does that guy think he is, anyway? . . . Imagine her daring to talk to me like that! . . . Man, the next time I see him, I'm going to sit him down and let him know exactly how I feel, and he's not going to like it one little bit.*

This went on for miles, and my usually buoyant spirit was fast dissipating under the weight of my wallowing in negative thinking. Here I was, a counselor committed to helping people work through the pain of their own emotional exhaustion and I was demonstrating the same behavior as those I'm committed to helping.

On the spot I made the decision to change my attitude. I picked up my pace and got my heart rate up. Then I said a prayer, asking God to forgive me for indulging in an attitude of despair and complaint. I started to count my blessings—thanking God for my wonderful wife, who has been my partner for so many years. I thanked the Father for the beautiful Northwest where I'm privileged to live. I started reciting the names of my friends who care about me and who had touched my life when I was at the brink of my own emotional exhaustion. I prayed for each of them, one by one, asking God to give them strength and courage and that they might always

---

Brisk walking, running, cycling, hiking—any kind of physical exercise that's challenging for you—can help you see your life's problems with new eyes and can, in fact, even alter your attitude.

---

have the inner resolve to be the persons our heavenly Father designed them to be.

By now I was cruising—picking 'em up, and laying 'em down. I scarcely remember the scenery, the rocks on the road, the traffic, or anything else on my run that day. Everything had suddenly come together for me—the physical, emotional, and spiritual—and it started by simply getting some exercise for my body. When I came home, I felt taller and stronger inside and out. Gone were my earlier complaints—still to be dealt with but now with a different attitude—and in their place was a spirit of gratitude.

We dare not underestimate the importance of physical activity in helping us to eliminate self-defeating attitudes. As mentioned in chapter 6, it's not necessary to purchase expensive equipment to exercise. We just need to get up, get out, and get moving. There are now scores of studies that confirm that exercise can be a direct antidote to stress. Whether a workout activates stress-destroying endorphins or simply provides for a relaxing pause in the action, we know that something good happens. Many times I've heard people say it's impossible to take your troubles on horseback. I guess that's because the troubles just bounce off—which would be particularly true the way *I* ride a horse! But I assure you it can be the same with any form of physical activity you choose where you push more blood to your heart, strengthen your muscles, increase your brain's alpha waves, and get the kind of juices flowing that make your body perform in the manner God intended.

Discipline 3—Become Accountable

An acquaintance I'll call Peter spends much of his time defending himself as a self-made man. Instead of a clothes brush, I think he may use a Brillo pad to clean the armor suit of cynicism he wears as he walks his daily road, which he does not realize can only lead to despair. He doesn't want to be "taken in" by resorting to the counsel of others, because he feels most people would not be bright enough or savvy enough to meet his higher standards. He considers anything that smacks of a team effort as demeaning.

Each day Peter dons his protective helmet and squeezes into his emotional chain mail and armored plates as he goes out, solo, sword of false self-assurance in hand, clanking through another day of stiffly meeting his obligations in punctureproof attire that shields him from his environment and from ever knowing there is more to life than being locked in a prison of fear. Peter, to this point, has still not learned the life-giving possibilities that come from being accountable to another human being, and I can only hope he makes more progress in seeing his self-imposed prison in the days ahead.

If we are to grow and develop healthy attitudes that will serve us for a lifetime, we need to share our despair, happiness, sorrow, and joy with a few trusted friends. We all need a friend or two who will be honest enough to tell it like it is. If, instead, we rely on pessimism, cynicism, or suspicion to shield ourselves from others, we'll find ourselves truly alone

---

If, instead, we rely on pessimism, cynicism, or suspicion to shield ourselves from others, we'll find ourselves truly alone one day— and in that hour, our aloneness may be more than we can bear.

---

one day—and in that hour, our aloneness may be more than we can bear.

Accountability keeps us on track. It prevents us from falling off steep cliffs. It provides an objective point of view when we've lost our ability to reason. Accountability reminds us we are not alone with our hurts and fears but that we are members of a fragile human race and that none of us is self-made.

We don't want to be like the little girl who was asked by her Sunday school teacher, "Who made you?" After much thought, the five-year-old answered, "Well, you know God made *part* of me." "What do you mean God made just *part* of you?" asked the teacher. "You see," the girl replied, "God made me really, really little, and then I just growed up all by myself the rest of the way."

Some day she'll understand, won't she? The bigger question is, when will we understand that success and winning in life is not a go-it-alone procedure. Self-defeating attitudes feed on the self-made-person syndrome—a lonely dead end. Ask yourself: To whom am I accountable? Am I wearing a protective, emotional armor that keeps me from loving others or being loved? If so, now is a good time to change your wardrobe so you can experience the freshness and exhilaration that come from a relationship of mutual understanding, honesty, and respect.

As we've already said, this kind of relationship requires love, acceptance, and forgiveness. Identify a person with whom you can build such a relationship. This person is probably someone already in your circle, perhaps in your church. To develop a reciprocal relationship of accountability with another person, you must believe in each other, encourage each other, honor each other, and serve each other. You must *allow* the friendship to develop over time. You can't force it, but there are things you can do: Try to spend time together doing fun things and learning new things, pray together, listen to each other, and be available to provide mutual support. At the same time you will need to give each other space and allow each other to grow. Developing intimacy *and* giving each other space are the ways to nurture a deep friendship of accountability, and accountability always plays a key role in recovering from emotional exhaustion.

Discipline 4—Learn to Be Content with What You Have

Wise men and women know that happiness comes from accepting the impossible, doing without the indispensable, and bearing the intolerable. Yet some of us allow our lack of contentment to so overpower us that we compromise our physical, mental, and spiritual health. Wouldn't we all have a better shot at happiness if we didn't place so many conditions on it? Sometimes it seems like a broken record as people come to me and tell me how they could be happy *if only* . . .

> If only my husband would lose some weight, then I'd be happy.
> If I just had another five hundred dollars a month, then I'd be happy.

If I just had a different spouse, then I'd be happy.

If I only had a nicer house, then I'd be happy.

If only I'd had more education, then I'd be happy.

When I start to have children, then I'll be happy.

If I didn't have so many children, then I'd be happy.

When my children leave home, then I'll really be happy.

The conditions we demand for happiness are often what keep us from being content. Unfortunately life is simply not fair, nor will it ever be. Justice will not always be served; tragedy will strike the innocent; the actions of the cruel will go unpunished. You and I may not approve of this singularly cavalier arrangement, but that's the way life is.

It takes only a cursory reading of the Book of Job to understand that the upright will feel the sharp end of the stick as often as the scoundrel. To believe and accept this as part of your belief system is to embark on a journey to peace, acceptance, and contentment. We do well to follow the example of the apostle Paul, who wrote in Philippians 4:11–13:

> I have learned to be content whatever the circumstances. I know what it is to be in need, and I know what it is to have plenty. I have learned the secret of being content in any and every situation, whether well fed or hungry, whether living in plenty or in want. I can do everything through him who gives me strength.

Discipline 5—Relinquish Your Anger

Men and women who are chronically angry face four to seven times the risk of dying of heart disease and cancer as those who are not prone to anger. Anger is a natural emotion (see chapter 3 for an in-depth discussion), but it is harmful when it becomes our focus or a continual part of our personality. Some anger is obvious, but there is also an inordinate amount of hidden anger lurking in the hearts, souls, and spirits of people. What we refuse to acknowledge, we cannot comprehend, and what we cannot understand, we cannot influence. To deal with the problem of anger, we must first be honest and open about the feelings we may have refused to acknowledge or tried to suppress.

Self-defeating attitudes are often symptoms of anger, mistrust, and self-hate, creating so much havoc with our self-esteem that it becomes impossible to see God's presence in our lives. It may be anger over the way you were treated as a child that continues to dog your steps as an adult. Or you may harbor anger stemming from a failed relationship, being fired from a job, being discriminated against because of your race or gender, or feeling that life has been unfair to you.

Anger enters our lives in many ways, but when we lock it up for fear of being honest with our feelings or from anxiety over possible reprisals, it does not go away. Instead, it grows inside the emotional walls until it becomes so strong it cannot be contained. For some, the anger seeps out slowly for years—deadly, toxic anger and discontent. For others, the power of the anger is so intense that it bursts all bonds, emerges as a flood, making us out-of-control terrors on the loose.

When you feel anger coming on, learn to ask yourself three simple questions:

1. Is this an issue of truly great importance?
2. Can I justify my anger in this situation?
3. Can I do anything right now to solve the problem?

If you can honestly answer *no* to these three questions, you should take this as a warning to slow down, calm down, and relax before you do anything that might hurt you or someone else. Ask yourself these three questions the next time you're stuck in traffic. Then, instead of steaming and fuming about the inevitable, put on a relaxing music tape, say a prayer, and thank God for your blessings. Learn to slow down and make good use of the time rather than letting your anger get the upper hand.

If you find you continue to hurt yourself and others with your anger, then you need to talk through your anger in a safe place with a counselor you trust. If you do not investigate your rage and resentment, you will set up insurmountable roadblocks that prevent you from traveling the path to inner healing. You need to recognize that your anger is essentially raw energy and a result of hurt, frustration, or fear. So get to the bottom of the real issues: What/who has hurt you? What/who is getting you all frustrated? What/whom do you fear? As you deal honestly with your anger and come to grips with it rationally, determine to use what was once anger energy to deal with the real issues at hand, which usually means dealing with unfinished business that can lead you out of the pain and sorrow of emotional exhaustion.

Discipline 6—Clean House Emotionally

In an effort to clean house emotionally, I would like to give you six "brooms" you can use to sweep your emotional house from stress and self-defeating attitudes:

1. *Learn to relax.* Often just thirty seconds of quiet, deep breathing, and prayer can give you the stamina you need to carry on with your day's work. I do this several times a day and I invite you to do the same. Make relaxing one of your major priorities. If you need to write *relax* in your daily planner, do it, and do it often. Take whatever steps are necessary

to slow down your busy life and you'll discover it will help you gain a new perspective on what is important.

2. *Don't be afraid to cry.* I have a cartoon in which a little boy is counseling his dog. The child says, "When you feel sad, you get little gray clouds inside your brain. When rain falls from those clouds, your head fills with water. That's where tears come from." Regardless of where your tears come from, let them come—whether you are a man or a woman. Crying is one of the ways God created for ridding the body of stress, through the outlet of tears. Over the years I've discovered that it actually takes a stronger person to cry than not to cry. Don't deny yourself this natural, drug-free opportunity to alleviate stress and exhaustion. If a movie makes you cry, don't choke back your tears; let them flow. When you read an article or story that touches you, go ahead and cry. It will refresh your soul.

3. *Give up perfectionism and admit to being human.* If you want to stay perpetually self-defeated, then demand perfection of yourself. You'll make yourself absolutely miserable. Recognizing you are not perfect does not mean you've thrown away your standards. It does mean you refuse to be paralyzed when life doesn't move according to your rhythm or plan. When actors get stage fright, it is usually because they think if their performance is less than perfect, they will have blown it for good. This mindset actually increases their anxiety. In the same way, we increase our stress when we mistakenly assume we are somehow inadequate if we ever make a mistake. Robert Eliot, director of the Institute of Stress Medicine in Jackson Hole, Wyoming, says professional women are prime candidates for perfectionist thinking. In his book *From Stress to Strength,* Eliot says many women feel they're fighting a biological clock and trying to get through the glass ceiling at the same time. He suggests we ask: Do all of these things really have to be the very best I can do? How about changing

I should, I must, and *I have to* to *it would be nice if....*[1] I assure you that your body will say thank you when you do.

4. *Do less.* Most of us simply try to cram too many activities into a finite number of hours. You don't need to see every movie, go to every sale, sign up for every class (for yourself

---

Recognizing you are not perfect does not mean you've thrown away your standards. It does mean you refuse to be paralyzed when life doesn't move according to your rhythm or plan.

---

or for your children), be on every committee at church, bowl every Thursday night, and work to develop a cure for cancer on the weekends. It's just too much.

You don't have to take my word for it. Make a list of all your activities. Then indicate after each item: *must do, sort of important,* or *can be put on hold.* Then use this list to determine which activities you can drop from your hectic schedule. If you don't take control of your activities, they will continue to rule your life, make you weak, and keep you emotionally exhausted. Ask yourself: Do I really need to watch that much TV? Could I spend more leisurely time with friends?

This concept can also apply to our vacations. Leave the cellular phone at home, and don't check your email. Don't pack your vacation with so many activities that you need to come home just to revive your worn-out spirits. The real at-ease vacation is time with family, lots of belly laughs, and not worrying about what you accomplish—along with a deep, quiet reflection on God's merciful kindness to you and to those you love.

5. *Adopt a pet.* You probably didn't think I'd put this one on the list, but I now am beginning to fully understand how important loving an animal can be in reducing stress. Yes, they get fleas, slobber all over, chew on or scratch your furniture, and mess up your carpet, but these are small prices to pay if

you want an in-house, faithful, relatively low maintenance, cost-effective stress buster. A survey of 5,471 Australians reported that those who owned pets had cholesterol and triglyceride levels markedly lower than those who did not own a pet. We now know that heart attack victims are more likely to be alive one year after their attack if they have an animal at their side. So whether you're into lizards, rottweilers, or Siamese cats, consider the therapeutic value of having a pet as your good buddy and stress reliever.

6. *Clean up the clutter and make a master list.* Most people seem to spend half their time looking for things in the midst of clutter, saying, "I know it's here someplace. Just give me a couple minutes, and I'll find it." Trouble is, those minutes add up to hours and days and weeks and eventually months of frustration. Clutter has the power to wear you down and make you weak. So I encourage you to clean your desk, tidy your room, organize the trunk of your car. As you remove the clutter, you'll begin to realize the joys of a better organized life. Now you can also remove the clutter from your schedule. Make a master list of what you really need to do. Put it on your computer and refer to it regularly. Or get a notebook and outline your priorities. One of the best times to review your master list is just before you retire at night. A job half organized is a job half done, and you'll discover that by morning you will have already thought your way through many of your projects.

Reflect, Renew, Rebuild

Reflect. Thomas Merton wrote, "For how can I receive the seeds of freedom if I am in love with slavery, and how can I cherish the desire of God if I am filled with another and an opposite desire?" What does this statement say to you in light of what you have just read in this chapter? What slavery might you still be in love with? How do you see yourself eliminating self-defeating habits as you work toward regaining control of your life?

Renew. Which of the six disciplines in this chapter have spoken most directly to your needs at this time? Write a couple of paragraphs in your journal that describe what you have learned from this chapter and how you will put this into action.

As you begin practicing the six disciplines, you will discover many wonderful things begin to happen in your life that help you refocus your priorities and reduce your level of emotional exhaustion. But just as the appearance of one robin does not promise a spring, so you must trust these disciplines for the long haul rather than expecting overnight success.

Rebuild. As you review what you've learned in this chapter, I encourage you to write these words on the tablet of your heart: God did not make me to live in frustration and defeat. He created me to sing his praises even in the center of some of the greatest storms of my life.

If you want to live life with joy and abandon, then attitudes of self-defeat and despair can only run counter to what you were created to be. Because of your persistence in determining to be all you can be, you are now one step further removed from your earlier state of emotional exhaustion and one step closer to inner healing. Congratulations on your progress. The good news is that the best for you and your life is yet to come.

8

The Joy of Confident Living

When confronted with a Goliath-sized dilemma, how do you respond: "He's too big to hit," or, like David, "He's too big to miss"?

We dare not wait for great strength before setting out to do our work, for to delay will weaken us further. Neither should we strain to see the end of the road before embarking on our journey, for every moment's hesitation eats at our confidence and erodes our courage. However, when we take our first tentative steps toward a worthy goal, rather than depleting our strength, we discover our power has increased manyfold and we see more clearly what our next task must be. This is because God's reward for a job well done is often a bigger job to do.

We Knew You'd Make It

Here are two stories of courage and confidence.

Stop Kvetching and Start Stretching

Judi, a reporter on an East Coast newspaper, lost her job in a large company layoff. Out of work and dejected, she fell into a three-month depression. Just getting up in the morning to wash her face and brush her teeth took more strength than she felt she could muster.

Judi began taking long, daily walks and praying for the ability to start being her own best friend—even asking God to teach her to compliment herself when she did a good job on the smallest of tasks. One day a friend sent her flowers with a note attached that read, "Hang in there. Stop *kvetching* and start stretching!"

Judi accepted this pointed counsel from her friend as a wake-up call and took the advice to heart. She started returning phone calls and began to develop her skills with a camera. Before long an editor called and offered her a freelance assignment. That one call was all the encouragement Judi needed to press on, even though there were many setbacks along the way. Her self-esteem grew to the point that she eventually developed the confidence to begin writing her own column for several leading Florida newspapers.

"I am stronger now because of the emotional and mental work I've done," Judi said. "Out of the lemons I was handed, I believe I've made a perfectly respectable lemonade." To this young writer we say, congratulations for hanging in there and for doing the hard work necessary to become strong again.

It's a Miracle I'm Here

Will, a long-distance bus driver, was spending thousands of dollars a month on his cocaine habit. He finally hit bottom when it was discovered he'd been stealing from his company. Out of work and down on his luck, for some reason Will decided to visit a local city college just to see what the academic world was like. "One thing for sure, I never thought of myself as college material," said the young man, "and God knows I had zero self-confidence. I couldn't believe it when one of the teachers I talked to actually told me that I'd make it."

And make it he did. Along with the required courses for his degree, Will disciplined himself in the study of substance abuse, while at the same time receiving treatment himself. By the time he received his first A, he was well on his way to overcoming his own addiction. At graduation Will was chosen valedictorian for his class. "It's a miracle I'm here," he said. "I could never have imagined this. Never." Later Will won a coveted scholarship and he plans to become a psychologist specializing in substance abuse.

Life seemed to have slammed its doors on Judi's and Will's hopes and dreams. But because someone believed in them, encouraged them, and told them they could do it, they took the risk to look beneath the surface and find their God-given potential, revealing untapped reserves of intelligence, giftedness, and imagination.

Fan into Flame Your Gift

I think 2 Timothy 1:6 sums up best the reason to hope: "For this reason I remind you to fan into flame the gift of God, which is in you." I suggest that you memorize these words of hope and confidence, and then consider them as the theme for this chapter. Being confident means you feel good about what is true about yourself. That's why the apostle Paul used the words "fan into flame the gift of God." Timothy's gift was already there. It didn't have to be fabricated. It's just that Timothy had not yet recognized what lay deep beneath his surface. Paul knew what he was talking about when he penned these words of confidence to his son in the faith. He recognized Timothy was inexperienced, timid, and afraid and that he often felt incapable of carrying out his ministry because of his youth. But Paul knew Timothy. He was confident that beneath the self-doubt there was the faithful heartbeat of one of God's chosen servants who would be used to make his Lord known.

Hundreds of years later Paul's words still have the power to bring hope to our hearts—if we will allow them to do their

---

Paul knew Timothy. He was confident that beneath the self-doubt there was the faithful heartbeat of one of God's chosen servants who would be used to make his Lord known.

---

good work in our lives. What gift has God given you that is waiting to emerge? Are you willing to take some small risks to discover the much greater, hidden treasures still buried deep within you? What will it take for you to develop the inner confidence to help you make your fondest dreams come true? Are you willing to take some risks—as Judi, Will, and young Timothy did—to propel you beyond the ordinary to do some truly amazing things with your life?

In his bestselling book, *Empires of the Mind*, Denis Waitley puts the issue of taking risks into perspective with a poem that, unfortunately, could be the epitaph for much of humanity:

> There was a very cautious man
> who never laughed or cried.
> He never risked, he never lost,
> he never won nor tried.
> And when one day he passed away
> his insurance was denied,
> for since he never really lived,
> they claimed he never died.

Waitley continues,

Missed opportunities are the curse of potential. Just after the Great Depression, Americans, perhaps understandably at the time, took many steps intended to minimize risk. The government guaranteed much of our savings. Citizens bought billions of dollars worth of insurance. We sought lifetime employment and our unions fought for guaranteed annual cost-of-living increases to protect us from inflation. This security-blanket mentality has continued in recent decades as executives awarded themselves giant golden parachutes in case a merger or takeover took their plum jobs.

These measures had many benefits, but the drawbacks have also been heavy, even if less obvious. In our eagerness to avoid risk, we forgot its positive aspects. Many of us continue to overlook the fact that progress comes only when chances are taken. And the security we sought and continue to seek often produces boredom, mediocrity, apathy, and reduced opportunity.[1]

People Who Refused to Quit

At some point in our lives, we all find ourselves burned out, emotionally exhausted, depressed, distressed, and afraid ever to risk again. Things don't work out as we think they should. Intimate relationships come to an end. Friends and family die, leaving us at a loss. Our children listen to their own drummers and couldn't care less about our core values. We lose our jobs, our courage, our timing, our hair, and our confidence. We've all been there more times than we'd like to admit. But the comforting news is that we are not alone, because this scourge of discouragement has plagued some of the most familiar names in history. Consider these individuals and the challenges they faced.

- Walt Disney was fired by a newspaper editor because he "lacked ideas." Disney went bankrupt several times before he developed a theme park now known as "the happiest place on earth."

- A diving accident in 1967 left Joni Eareckson Tada a quadriplegic. Gradually Joni discovered a personal joy and peace in God so powerful that her life now inspires thousands worldwide. A talented vocalist, artist, and writer, she is a leading advocate for disabled persons.

- An "expert" said of football great Vince Lombardi, "He possesses minimal football knowledge and lacks motivation."

- The mother and father of the famed opera singer Enrico Caruso wanted him to have a career in engineering. His teachers said he had no voice at all and simply could not sing.

- Albert Einstein did not speak until he was four years old. He didn't read until he was seven. His teacher described young Albert as "mentally slow, unsociable, and adrift forever in his foolish dreams." He was expelled and was refused readmittance to the Zurich Polytechnic School.

- Louisa May Alcott, author of *Little Women*, was told by her family that it might be best if she'd look for work as a servant or seamstress.

- Jackie Robinson, grandson of a slave and abandoned at six years of age by his father, broke the color barrier in baseball and was voted the National League's most valuable player in 1949.

- John Bunyan, while languishing in an English prison for twelve years for preaching in nonsanctioned places, wrote *Grace Abounding* and *Confessions of Faith* and began formulating his major work, *Pilgrim's Progress*.

- Leo Tolstoy, author of *War and Peace*, failed college. His teachers considered him "both unable and unwilling to learn."
- Babe Ruth, arguably the greatest athlete of all time and famous for setting the home run record also held the record for most strikeouts.
- Winston Churchill flunked sixth grade. He did not become prime minister of England until age sixty-two, and then only after a lifetime of defeats and missed opportunities. The greatest contributions he made to his country and the free world came when he was a senior citizen.
- After Fred Astaire's first screen test, the memorandum from the MGM testing director, dated 1933, read, "Can't act. Slightly bald. Can dance a little." Astaire kept that memo over the fireplace in his Beverly Hills home.

What made these people—once considered failures— persevere despite insurmountable odds? It wasn't their education, their good looks, or, in most cases, even their IQ. It was something less tangible. There was something different in their spirit that set them apart. Let's look together at some of the characteristics of their lives that gave them the confidence to move in the direction of their dreams. If we emulate these characteristics, we will be on our way to becoming strong again.

1. *They faced their fears—and conquered them.* We now believe there are only two inherent fears: the fear of falling and fear of loud noises. Yet there have been psychological tests given to large numbers of people in which seven thousand fears were identified—all acquired. Most of us develop our confidence by confronting our anxieties and discouragements and determining to do what we have set out to do. When you admit that most of your fears are homegrown, you can then

make the decision to stop feeding them, pull them up by the roots, and regain control of your life.

2. *They stayed focused and flexible and they had fun!* These three attributes will move you closer to your dreams than anything else: focus, flexibility, fun. They will help you do your job with greater confidence, provide you with more wisdom, and make you a more resilient person. Success will probably

---

When you admit that most of your fears are homegrown, you can then make the decision to stop feeding them, pull them up by the roots, and regain control of your life.

---

not come your way overnight. Progress takes time. Achieving anything of significant value not only takes long hours, but it also demands long periods of courage and stamina.

3. *They refused to give up on their dreams.* Whenever we have a dream, we must realize that there will invariably be dream snatchers lurking in the most unsuspecting places. They may be well-meaning family, colleagues at work, or even those we thought would be the most enthusiastic cheerleaders for our new venture. Surprise! Sometimes we find we're all alone with our dreams. That's how Jackie Robinson, Louisa May Alcott, Walt Disney, Joni Eareckson Tada, Leo Tolstoy, and the rest of our parade of heroes felt on more than one occasion. What do you do when people throw water on your ambitions or arrange for rain on the afternoon of your parade? As you ask God to program you with his confidence, you will learn to accept these individuals as temporary obstacles around which you must either walk or run. Never allow them to determine your direction.

4. *They maintained a spirit of optimism.* The Bible says as a person thinks, so is he (see Proverbs 23:7). To develop a spirit of confidence and optimism, we need to establish and maintain a godly enthusiasm about our goals and dreams and

see them as already coming true. To do this, we will give up all things that oppose our goals, focus deliberately on what we want to accomplish, and desire it above all else. What is

---

What do you do when people throw water on your ambitions or arrange for rain on the afternoon of your parade?

---

your burning desire? What would you attempt if you knew you could not fail? God is calling you to some act of service, and in his sight it is neither too great nor too small.

5. *They thought with their hearts.* Victor Hugo said, "An invasion of armies can be resisted, but not an idea whose time has come." The amount of thinking required for you to move in the direction of your dreams and see them become reality may vary from project to project. But when you are confident what you are doing is right and that it has God's blessing, you will get the job done regardless of the amount of thinking time it takes. Leonardo da Vinci thought through and designed the helicopter on paper four hundred years before the first chopper lifted off the ground. Edison thought through the concepts of the phonograph, electric light, an improved telephone, and moving pictures and then turned them into reality. As you allow God to direct your thoughts and ask him to anoint your

---

An invasion of armies can be resisted,
but not an idea whose time has come.
Victor Hugo

---

desires, he will give you the insight and wisdom you need to see your dreams come true.

6. *They used their stumbling blocks as stepping-stones.* Scott Stuart had been a lifeguard for sixteen years when he became a quadriplegic after a diving accident. Now he works as a

lifeguard dispatcher. With every logical reason to be depressed and to see himself as incapable of following his dreams, Scott has instead made it his goal to make the beaches of California accessible to those in wheelchairs through sand-traction surf chairs. He's already begun a campaign for what he believes "will be one more step toward independence for all disabled people." When you accept your setbacks as stepping-stones rather than stumbling blocks, you will become stronger and wiser and you'll discover you are a person who understands the joy of living confidently.

When you make the decision to accept God's strength as your strength—even if you must do it without the approval or understanding of others—you will radiate confidence, because your spirit will be too large for worry, too courageous for fear, and too happy to allow the seeds of trouble to take root in your life.

It's Not Failure at All

I make it a point to listen to as many audiotapes and read as many books as possible by John Maxwell, one of the finest Christian leaders and communicators today. Maxwell speaks the truth and describes it in ways that are unforgettable. About *failure* he says that we should not be ashamed of what may appear to be failure because it often means we

---

As you allow God to direct your thoughts and ask him to anoint your desires, he will give you the insight and wisdom you need to see your dreams come true.

---

had courage to try something different, we learned new information, and we now have a better idea of how it should be done. In other words, what some people call failure, we can call a learning experience.

If what we call *failure* is never final but simply a means of getting closer to our goals, then it stands to reason that the best book has not yet been written. The most beautiful concerto has not yet been composed. The most energy-efficient car has yet to come off the production line. The most effective cancer cure has not yet been developed in the laboratory. And the better *you* has yet to emerge.

I want to offer you a challenge: What are you willing to do, starting today, to ratchet up your confidence a notch or two? What can you tackle right now to help you deal with your

---

What can you tackle right now to help you deal with your challenges in ways you never thought possible? How can you make your most intimate relationships better and stronger?

---

challenges in ways you never thought possible? How can you make your most intimate relationships better and stronger? How can you revisit old attitudes, and perhaps revise them, to help you reach out to those in need in creative, new ways?

To help you brainstorm on this, I invite you to get out your journal and write your responses to the following:

1. Choose one specific thing to work on immediately that will help you know the joy of living confidently. Describe your objective and how you plan to accomplish it.
2. Identify the habitual ways of thinking that have been holding you back, making you afraid, and keeping you from believing your dreams will come true.
3. Based on what you have learned so far in this chapter, write down what you plan to do to make life's circumstances adjust to your dreams and not the other way around.

4. Reflect on the Chinese proverb, "Flowers leave part of their fragrance in the hands that bestow them." Write your thoughts in your journal.

5. What is your primary response to the statement, "Becoming more comfortable with myself is a strong sign of growth and inner confidence"?

6. In the past you have often used unreliable maps and timetables and have even chosen nonsupportive traveling companions at times. Write what you now know you must do to find inner healing.

7. Reflect on this Kenyan prayer: "From the cowardice that dares not face new truths; from the laziness that is content with half-truths; from the arrogance that thinks it knows all truths, dear God, deliver me."

8. When you exchange your mistakes for wisdom and increased confidence, you make an excellent trade because you now know what?

9. What are three fears that have kept you from being confident about your God-given potential?

10. What do you intend to do immediately about these three fears as you develop the confidence to regain control of your life?

11. Always remember that God loves you and forgives you whether you are able to exude confidence or not at this place in your life. In your own words, write a thank-you to God for how much he loves you and for his desire that you use his strength to find inner healing.

Choose Your Battles Carefully

As you work deliberately to develop confidence in your daily living, I urge you to concern yourself with the things you can harness rather than issues that are beyond your control.

Perhaps it's your futile attempts to conquer every one of your challenges that have burned you out, bringing you to the edge of emotional exhaustion. While it is noble to believe you possess the requisite resources to solve each problem that arises in your life, it's probably not too realistic. You simply cannot do it all. Do only what you can do at first. Then follow your small successes with small risks, which will further increase your confidence and eventually make you strong.

You may need to start with eliminating extraneous information about events and people that are beyond your influence to

---

Television may seem to be a relaxing behavior——40 percent of Americans' leisure time is spent glued to the tube. Yet studies indicate that we actually feel less relaxed and satisfied after a few hours watching TV than we did before.

---

change—which may mean reducing the amount of television you watch with its stories of economic turmoil, mayhem, and murder. Television may seem to be a relaxing behavior—40 percent of Americans' leisure time is spent glued to the tube. Yet studies indicate that we actually feel less relaxed and satisfied after a few hours watching TV than we did before.

Ask yourself: Where should the lines of battle be drawn in my life? What activities can I jettison to make room for things and people that will nourish my spirit? Where should I put my energies so that I do not dissipate my strength?

Adventure and Significance

Betty came to see me in my office and explained that she had suddenly come to a critical turning point in her life. She had worked with enthusiasm for many years as a secretary in a leading law firm but was now obliged by circumstances beyond her control to leave her position. It was not going to be easy for Betty to leave her friends, her boss, and the corporate culture that had become such an integral part of her life. She worried that she would not find a position elsewhere that would be as fulfilling and interesting. If she turned to a different occupation, even for a short time, Betty would run the risk of finding it difficult ever to return to the kind of *adventure*—a word she used often in our conversation—she had been engaged in for so long.

I asked her, "What do you want most of all in the world?" There was a long silence. Then Betty replied, "I want to do something truly significant with my life."

Something significant. We talked for more than an hour about the meaning of those words. What does it mean, "something significant"? Is anything ever ultimately significant? Betty hopes so. In fact she is counting on it.

As a counselor I must be careful not to lay on Betty my value judgments of what may or may not be significant for her. If I were to do so, I would be treating her as less than a capable, responsible person. What she needs from me more than anything else is a dialogue. Few people learn to understand themselves in isolation. Understanding comes only in deep encounters with others.

Betty broke the silence, "I know that just because something is good, it will not necessarily be significant. But I'm confident that if I can be and do significant things, I know that what I put my heart to will be good."

Did you catch the word Betty used earlier in our conversation—the word *adventure*? Life for this woman has always been adventure—complete with hills and valleys, storms and sunsets, hurts and passion. Once a person without a shred of confidence, weak and ineffective, she learned that it has been through her adventures that she has become the mature woman she is today. Each passing has made her available for other adventures, which have always been more adult and more fruitful. Now another adventure awaits her.

I tell you Betty's story because our lives cry out for adventure and significance. That's why we climb mountains, swim in high surf, extreme ski, scuba dive, fly airplanes, go on vacations to exciting places. It's why we sit wide-eyed with our hearts pounding through our chests as the roller coaster approaches its final ascent just before it leaps into space, where for those few out-of-body moments we can scarcely catch our breath as our hearts fall to our stomachs and we're lost in the thrill of temporary weightlessness, screaming, blood

---

Fan into flame the gift of God that is in you. Remember the source of your strength. Aim for excellence, not for perfection, and confidence will be yours.

---

pressure rising, with adrenaline coursing through our bodies faster than a moving train. Our spirits cry out for these thrills as an escape from our humdrum existence.

The good news is that you and I can have the kind of daily confidence in ourselves that makes real adventures happen in the here and now. It's not necessary for us to wait until we can get to the nearest theme park to pay our money, stand in line, and get our thrills. The things we've spoken of in this chapter are the nuts and bolts of confidence-building that will help you recognize and enjoy some of the greatest adventures you will ever experience.

I say this with confidence because even though I have never met you, I know what you want in your heart of hearts. You, like Betty, want to be significant, and you want to do significant things. Your adventures will help define your significance as much as anything else because they are manifestations of your self-expression. Your adventures will invigorate you, push you beyond yourself, and propel you toward your worthy goals. They will demand that you risk stepping out of the too-safe shallows into the wild white water of life where the real action is, where you will encounter both the exhilaration of victory and the learning that comes from defeat.

So press on with confidence. Stay around people who will help you grow. Accentuate the positive. Fan into flame the gift of God that is in you. Remember the source of your strength. Aim for excellence, not for perfection, and confidence will be yours. I invite you to live boldly and confidently with this assurance.

—— *Reflect, Renew, Rebuild* ——

Reflect. When you recognize the true source of your strength and allow God to touch your life, you will demonstrate a confidence that will move you away from exhaustion, unleash your gifts and, in turn, make you a confidence-giver to others. William Jennings Bryan wrote, "If the Father deigns to touch with divine power the cold and pulseless heart of the buried acorn and to make it burst forth from its prison walls, will he have neglected in the earth the soul of man made in the image of his Creator?" With this chapter as your reference point, how do you respond to Bryan's statement?

Renew. In this chapter we have looked together at some of the key ingredients necessary to live confidently—including never permitting failure to become a habit. Take a moment and consider your present circumstances. Where in your life would you like more confidence? How would you feel and act if you had this confidence. "Be strong, be brave, and do not be afraid. . . . We have the Lord our God to fight our battles for us!" (2 Chron. 32:7, 8 TLB).

Rebuild. To begin to build confidence in your daily life, it's important that you take immediate action in those areas that once shackled you and kept you from enjoying your God-given freedom. Here are five areas in which you may still be struggling. If so, write in your journal how you are going to build the kind of confidence necessary to deal with that issue in the days ahead.

1. I have often allowed difficult events and unhappy people in my past to drag me down.
2. I have often been afraid to take risks and have spoiled my present moments with anxiety about the future.
3. I have been more of a worrier than a doer, but now I recognize that worry has not served me well. It has made me weak and emotionally exhausted.
4. For too long I have allowed my life's circumstances to shape my attitude, and I have permitted misery to overshadow my joy.
5. I have indulged in too much self-pity and have often forgotten the biblical admonition to rejoice always and give thanks in all circumstances (see Philippians 4:4–6).

9

Living Right-Side Up
in an Upside-Down World

*The shadows will always be behind you
if you walk toward the light.*

Anonymous

The cheetah has extremely long legs and uses its heavy tail for *balance* when executing sharp turns.

When a state of equilibrium exists where no nation or group of nations is able to dominate others, we have achieved a vital *balance* of power.

Vertigo is a hallucination in which the individual or his or her surroundings seem to be spinning, in what may be experienced as a sensation of imminent loss of consciousness or absence of *balance*.

The violin section of a symphonic orchestra requires greater numbers to *balance* the corresponding viola, cello, and bass sections.

Like all Hebrew poetry, the psalms are written in parallel lines that *balance* words, images, and thoughts. They have the effect of creating special nuances and emphasizing the message through a skilled mixture of repetition and variation.

Balance, balance, balance. Beasts of the jungle have it. Politicians know they need it. Our bodies do not function well without it. Orchestras cannot produce a high quality sound if they don't have it. And the Jews knew that it would enhance their message and give their poetry a beauty and quality that would endure for generations.

Yet you and I just don't get it. We know we need to live balanced lives, but we tend not to. We go off on extremes and expect things to right themselves. We look back into history and see how most ancient cultures viewed balance as one of the most important ingredients for living effective lives. The Chinese, for example, fought against extremes in their ancient political philosophy and in their approach to health and, like the Hebrews, made balance a critical element in their poetry. But how do you and I stay topside up in a world intent on standing us on our heads, afflicting us with emotional vertigo, and encouraging the bass sections of our lives to drown out the violins?

The Fine Art of Maintaining Balance

In this chapter, you will find practical answers that will help you move away from emotional exhaustion. If you try to live without balance, you will invariably retreat to older patterns of thinking. The tendency is always to default to previous, often unbalanced, behavior when the going gets rough, when feeling boxed in, or when the pressures of life become more than you feel you can bear. But when you are armed with principles of fortification to help you predict the obstacles, know how to prevent them from disabling you, and realize you do not have to relapse, then you will be miles down the road to becoming strong and staying strong.

High stress is a prime cause of emotional imbalance and may even set you up for accidental injury and illness. Here is a useful set of questions to determine your stress level.

To help determine your current level of stress, answer the following questions based on the past six months. Keep a tally of the number of points for each *yes* answer.

	points
1. Has your husband or wife died?	20
2. Have you divorced or separated from your husband or wife?	15
3. Has a close relative died (other than your husband or wife)?	13
4. Have you been hospitalized?	11
5. Have you married or had a reconciliation with your partner after separation?	10
6. Have you found out you were soon to become a parent?	9
7. Has there been a change in the health of a close family member (good or bad)?	9
8. Have you lost a job or retired?	9
9. Are you having sexual difficulties?	8
10. Has a new member been born or married into your family?	8
11. Has a close friend died?	8
12. Have your finances become better or worse?	8
13. Have you changed your job?	8
14. Have any children moved out of the home or started/finished school?	6

15. Is trouble with in-laws causing trouble in your family? 6

16. Is there anyone at home or work you dislike strongly? 6

17. Do you frequently have premenstrual tension? 6

18. Have you had important personal success (such as a job promotion)? 6

19. Have you had "jet lag" (travel fatigue) at least twice? 6

20. Have you had a major domestic upheaval such as a move or remodeling of your home? 5

21. Have you had problems at work that may be putting your job at risk? 5

22. Have you taken on a large debt or mortgage? 3

23. Have you had a minor brush with the law (i.e., traffic violation)? 2

Evaluation: The higher your score, the more stressful your life. As a general guide, a score of thirty suggests you are not likely to have a stress-related illness or accidental injury now or in the near future. Challenges begin as you move up the point scale. If your score is sixty or more, your life is extremely stressful and you are at a higher risk for one or more stress-related illnesses. You also need to carefully evaluate decisions you make that may add to your stress.

Let me remind you that the above scale is not to be taken as final arbiter of your emotional health but only to give you a sense of why you may feel some of the strain you are experiencing at this time. These questions are not intended to cause fear but rather to help you understand your stress so you can get a firmer grasp on what may be the cause of your emotional exhaustion.

With this as backdrop, let's look at five key areas where you can fortify your life, create greater opportunities for emotional balance, and put yourself on track to stay right-side up in an upside-down world.

1. Create and Maintain Healthy Relationships

Healthy people are growing people, and people do not grow healthy in isolation. Let me give you an example of an executive I'll call Tom who tried to do it the other way around.

Tom didn't realize it at the time, but his success in climbing to a top executive position with his company was achieved at the expense of his personal life. Tom stayed at the office well into the evening each day, spent hundreds of hours on airplanes each year—always working madly on his laptop computer, of course—entertained clients over dinner, and took at least two full briefcases home each weekend. When Tom wasn't working, work was working Tom. Even when physically present at the family dinner table, his mind was still in the office, thinking of the current project, the next

> *When Tom wasn't working, work was working Tom.*
> *Even when physically present at the family dinner*
> *table, his mind was still in the office, thinking of the cur-*
> *rent project, the next project, or past projects.*

project, or past projects. When he'd go on vacations with his family, Tom would pack an extra box or two of business reports, books, and magazines. He never got to all of them but he was content to know that his security blankets were not far away.

This obsession with work was destroying Tom's relationship with his wife and children but it didn't seem to matter much to Tom, because he continued to get reinforcement for his yeoman efforts from his boss and colleagues. People in the office would say, "You know, Tom is just about the hardest-working guy I've ever seen in this place. I can't believe it. How does he do it? He keeps his weight down, has energy to spare, works until seven every night, comes in on Saturdays more than anyone else, works at home. What a guy!"

What a guy indeed. Although he says he loves his wife, Tom is now divorced, lives in a one-bedroom efficiency apartment, and misses his kids, but he is still nowhere near understanding what really happened. He tried to grow in one dimension only, and because of his physical endurance, business acumen, and the reinforcement he received from his colleagues, he figured he'd be able to pull it off.

Tom made his choice early on. He accepted the challenge to make work his life and life his work. He bought into reaping the benefits he thought he wanted, rewards he was sure would result from hard work and dedication: power, respect, money, and achievement. As advancements came his way, along with greater responsibility, the pressure to produce even more only increased.

Tom mistook an organized, effective, well-paid, well-oiled economic situation for a relationship. It was not. It was an arrangement for business purposes. Yes, Tom had to work and he was good at what he did. But there was no balance to his life. Tom had a loving wife and great kids who were dying to have a relationship with their husband and father. They needed to be recognized, uplifted, talked to, listened to. They needed—and still need—someone who regards their opinion as important and who will be there when they need him most.

Do you relate to Tom? You may have been on one end of the spectrum or the other. You may even now be so preoccupied with business success, travel, and the next deal that you are forgetting what may be most important in your life. Or you may be the one at home who wonders if your husband or wife will ever see the need for the kind of relationship you are eager to share. Remember that the most effective way of establishing healthy relationships with others is to become emotionally healthy yourself. It may involve some

---

Remember that the most effective way of establishing healthy relationships with others is to become emotionally healthy yourself.

---

serious challenges as you move through the process, but you must not forget the importance of your own emotional well-being.[1]

The following questions can help you recognize if you are creating and maintaining healthy relationships:

Am I able to slow down? Can I get rid of my dysfunctional attitudes about time that make me think I need to do everything now, in a hurry, at all costs, to the detriment of the relationships I say are important to me?

Am I looking at the bigger picture? Is what I do really what I want to do and be? Am I engaging in the kinds of activities that encourage or inhibit my relationships?

Am I equating work with my worth? It's been said that *we've become walking résumés,* meaning that we are what we do—no more, no less. Am I able to do something like walk on a secluded beach and enjoy a sunset with my spouse or a friend (without my cell phone or pager) and still feel I have value?

Do I take breaks during the day to do something besides work? Do I take the time to call a friend, take a five-minute vacation, write a love note or postcard to a son or daughter in college, or pick up some flowers for a loved one on my lunch break?

If your answers to these questions are generally *no*, it may be wise to share your concerns and observations with a friend, your pastor, or a professional counselor.

2. Learn to Become Pride and "Big" Ego Free

The Bible says, "Pride goes before destruction, a haughty spirit before a fall" (Prov. 16:18). *The Book of Common Prayer* pleads, "From pride, vain-glory, and hypocrisy; from envy,

---

It is not that we do great and marvelous things but that we are, as Oswald Chambers says, "good in motive because we have been made good by the supernatural grace of God."

---

hatred, and malice, and all uncharitableness, good Lord, deliver us." Daniel Defoe wrote, "Pride is the first peer and president of Hell."

For us who say we are disciples, it is not that we do great and marvelous things but that we are, as Oswald Chambers says, "good in motive because we have been made good by the supernatural grace of God."

To find inner healing, to maintain a healthy balance, and to avoid relapsing into old, ineffective patterns of behavior, we need to be willing to turn loose many of our external images and allow our faith to take us to the next step of emotional growth. Mahatma Gandhi wrote, "Many could forego heavy meals, a full wardrobe, a fine house, etc.; it is the ego they cannot forego." We have all accumulated so many trappings during our lives—externals that manifest themselves in how we relate to our money, our homes, the success of our children, our position in the community, and the way we wield power in the pulpit or the boardroom. The more strongly attached we remain to outward appearances of success, the more difficult it will be to move away from feeling emotionally exhausted. To determine whether this is a problem for you, ask yourself these three questions:

Am I overly attached to something because it puffs my ego and makes me look good to others, like a new car or a fashionable wardrobe?

Am I willing to take a small risk by looking at one area in my life where pride reigns supreme and begin to see it as a gift to share with others rather than a trophy about which to brag?

Am I willing to play armchair archaeologist and dig beneath my surface through the debris of hurt feelings and pain to discover who I really am?

What are you evaluating right now about your life? Are your pride and ego getting in the way of some remarkable things God wants to do to you, with you, and for you? Until now you've been adding more years to your life and that may have been about it. But when you take this principle and put it to work, you will begin to put more life to your years as you recover from emotional exhaustion.

3. Share Freely the Loves of Your Life

What are the loves of your life? I'm not talking about people here but rather about the things you truly love to do—your hobbies and interests. It may be your personality, your ability to keep them laughing for hours with your gift of humor, your skill at conversation. Perhaps it's your compassion for those in need. It may be how you relate to children, to the elderly, to the homeless. These are all part of your emotional DNA—the unique twists and turns that make you the special person you are.

Perhaps you've been emotionally exhausted for so long that you've put your loves on a shelf. Depression may have kept you isolated and afraid. You may have actually forgotten what once got you excited about life. Perhaps the model

---

You may have once had a smile as broad as all outdoors,
but your life's circumstances have taken your smile away.
It's not that you don't want to smile, but rather you feel
you no longer have much about which to smile.

---

train you used to have on display for the neighborhood kids to enjoy is gathering dust in your attic. At one time you loved photography but now you don't even know where your camera is. You may have once had a smile as broad as all outdoors, but your life's circumstances have taken your smile away. It's not that you don't want to smile, but rather you feel you no longer have much about which to smile.

I have a wonderful uncle who started making carvings for members of our family several years ago. Uncle Glenn is terrific at his craft, especially in carving little wooden cars that are so intricate they look like you could almost drive them. I can still see his broad smile as he took out a car and handed it to me as his special gift. Making these wood carvings for his family is one of the great loves of Uncle Glenn's life—a living, loving hobby that continues to create a ripple effect of love and affection.

Then there's my grandfather—a miner who owned silver and gold mines in Idaho. One of his loves was to pan for gold and to use the nuggets he found to make necklaces for the women in our family. These were handmade, pure gold nugget-laden necklaces—beautiful, personal works of art. But more than that, they were labors of love and gifts straight from my grandfather's heart. From the day he gave one to my wife as a present, I have never seen her without it. The day he died of Lou Gehrig's disease, my mother sat singing to him at his bedside, the gold nugget necklace around her neck reflecting the light from an open window. Today that heartfelt gift keeps on giving, bringing joy to the wearer and to all who see and appreciate this love-made piece of jewelry.

I tell you these two stories to encourage you to look deep within and beneath the mountain of hurt that may have buried some of your great loves. You certainly don't have to be a wood carver or a gold miner. That's not the point. It's not the cleverness of the gift but the attitude of the heart that gives the gift that matters. I'm confident there is something you may have put aside—a real love of your life—that you may now be ready to revisit, bring to the surface, and share with others.

Expressing the loves of your life again will help steady your course, because it will take your eyes away from yourself and focus them on others. This is something you must decide to do because it's the right thing for you to do—not as an ego trip or to impress someone else. When you give the gift of yourself freely, without thought of the cost—anything from your great smile, to baking a cake for someone, to making a gold nugget necklace—you will be edging closer to finding inner healing.

4. Nothing Is Etched in Stone

On my desk at The Center in Edmonds, Washington, is a beautiful, flat rock. Carved into this rock that I use as a paperweight are the words, "Nothing is etched in stone." I keep this motto in front of me as a reminder that God has given me an overwhelming sense of freedom to exercise many different options every day of my life. I can choose to do some things and choose not to do others. Nothing is etched in stone. I can work six hours or ten hours or choose not to work at all and take a vacation: Nothing is etched in stone.

I can save my money, spend my money, or waste my money. I can choose to spend time with one friend and not with another. I can make a decision to write one or two books a year, do a series of seminars on any number of topics, do something entirely different, or do nothing at all.

We are able to explore so many options because God has laid down laws and principles that do not put us in bondage but, when followed, give us freedom. Take the laws of gravity for instance. It may bind us to the earth but it also gives us the freedom to jog, cycle, work at a computer, enjoy a cup of coffee, cuddle a baby in our arms, or walk hand-in-hand with someone we love.

Some may see the Ten Commandments as repressive rules that take away our freedom. But how many of us would want to live in a world where it is totally acceptable to lie, steal, and

---

Once we can believe the truth that God is love and that he loves us more than we can ever love ourselves, we will be released from former bondage to live life with a new, positive orientation.

---

murder? Each of God's laws and principles are born of his love for us. Once we can believe the truth that God is love and that he loves us more than we can ever love ourselves, we will be released from former bondage to live life with a new, positive orientation.

Within the framework of God's laws and love, we are free to choose our options and to be creative. Past mistakes or abuse do not determine our future. We can choose to improve damaged relationships, change our appearance, expand our mind, or overcome past abuse.

God did not make us to be emotionally exhausted. With his help we can do better than that. We can pray for courage to be the person God designed us to be, and our prayers can be answered—because nothing is etched in stone except God's love for us.

5. God Prevails

At the very heart of maintaining our stability and balance must be this belief: God prevails. Whatever we do for good or ill, God prevails. After our best laid plans have been organized and implemented, God prevails. When we've done our homework, paid our dues, and sit back to wait for things to go our way because we deserve a break today, God prevails.

As I sit here at my desk writing these words on a yellow legal pad, my mind shoots back to fourteen years earlier when I was also sitting in this room. LaFon and I were newlyweds and we had just started The Center for Counseling and Health Resources. We began our counseling ministry even though many thought it was a foolish attempt that would go nowhere. For us, however, it was an act of faith as we opened our practice with only one room—the office in which I now sit.

We had nothing but these four walls. No waiting room, no amenities—and not that many clients for that matter. We were just two young people with a dream to reach out to individuals

---

God prevails during our moments of courage and he prevails in the dark night of our souls with its many fears and doubts.

---

and families struggling to keep their balance during difficult times. I wonder if we would have taken so many risks had we known what it takes to make dreams come true: the painful days of burnout and emotional exhaustion, the months when too many clients chose not to pay their bills, the times when LaFon and I would look at each other and wonder aloud if it was worth the effort.

But through it all we believed in our hearts that God would prevail. We knew he would rule in our successes and in our failures, and he did. Today we can say that he prevails when it rains and he prevails when we are blinded by the light of the morning sun. He prevails when you and I love and he prevails when we play God by trying to get our own way. God prevails during our moments of courage and he prevails in the dark night of our souls with its many fears and doubts.

Dr. Robert Schuller's prayers have helped sustain me for many years. I especially appreciate the ones in which he prays that God will not make our lives easier but rather that he will turn our fears around, making our most frightening moments the raw substance from which hope is created.

Healthy Balance or Balancing Act?

Do you ever get the feeling that God is the fisherman and you are the fish swimming madly away trying to avoid the hook? You see it coming, and you dodge it. *Whew! Escaped one more time.* After all, you think you have a better idea. You've developed your own way to regain control of your life. You have a unique method of creating balance in your life. However, you soon learn that the more you dodge his relentless pursuit, the deeper you descend into a weakness of spirit. Instead of getting it all together, life begins falling apart. What seemed like freedom and balance was really a balancing act, good for a few thrilling moments, but difficult to sustain—and especially frightening when you find yourself in the murky ocean depths.

Sometimes we are so weak and emotionally exhausted we feel we don't deserve to find healing because we are unworthy of God's attention. We even catch ourselves sabotaging our own progress. God says he loves us, but our lowered self-esteem keeps us from believing it.

If this is where you are today, it will be a challenge for you to remember and embrace the magnitude of God's love for you. It's what happens to all of us when we've lived on the other side of his love for so long. We've had lifestyles in which others abused us or we abused them. Sometimes this made us feel powerful; at other times we felt incredibly weak and ashamed.

Our backgrounds have not always prepared us to receive God's love and mercy, but that's what faith and hope are all about: accepting God's compassion while we're still in the pit, when we don't, can't, and even won't understand it. Your assignment, if you choose to accept it, is simply to get out of the way and let God love you, flood you with his compassion, and prevail in every area of your life. It's what will help you regain your balance and help you live right-side up in an upside-down world.

—————— *Reflect, Renew, Rebuild* ——————

Reflect. Let this prayer sweep over your spirit. After you've meditated on it for a few moments, make some notes in your journal on what it means to you in light of this chapter.

> Lord, I need only one thing in this world: To know myself, and to love You. Give me, heavenly Father, your love and

your peace. Help me do more than just survive this world of turmoil and fears. Make me strong. Keep me balanced. With these I am rich enough and desire nothing more. Dear Father in heaven, make my heart like yours. Amen.

Renew. Review the story of Tom and how his life unraveled because he remained out of balance, giving his entire efforts over to the acquisition of money, power, and prestige. Then consider your own life and your personal balancing act. Write in your journal three ways in which you are beginning to look at the bigger picture for your life.

Rebuild. I invite you to write a simple prayer of thanksgiving to God. Express your gratitude to the One who promises to relieve you from your emotional exhaustion. Thank him— even in advance, if necessary—for helping you regain your balance and the strength to live right-side up in an upside-down world.

10

Staying Emotionally Strong
in a Stress-Filled World

Life without idealism is empty indeed.
We must have hope or starve to death.

Pearl Buck

He was a sickly child, this boy from California. He was also small for his age. When he finally got to high school, he was still in poor health and only ninety-seven pounds soaking wet. He was so distraught by his size and health that he seldom dated. The girls had already pretty much declared him a social disaster waiting to happen and would have nothing to do with him. I imagine the arch supports, thick glasses, and shoulder brace didn't much help his chances either.

He finally threw in the towel, quit school, and mumbled something about the despair he'd probably face the rest of his life. Then one day while wandering aimlessly around his neighborhood, he stopped in to hear a health lecture. The ninety-seven-pound weakling got inspired by the message of hope he heard and decided, *If it is to be, it's up to me.* On the spot he made a decision to make some changes in his life.

Amazingly to those around him, he became a believer in self-determination. No more lousy nutrition for this boy. Junk food was out; good, healthy, life-sustaining food was in. He started to exercise two hours a day to strengthen his weak, skinny body. At first, he could hardly pick up a ten-pound dumbbell, but before long he was lifting heavy weights. With a sense of renewed confidence in himself and his future, he reentered high school.

The boy named Jack Lalanne was on the road to a healthy and brilliant career in bringing health to millions of Americans. He has been the recipient of many awards worldwide and is still known as Mr. Exercise. I'm sure you have heard the stories of how as a senior citizen he continues to run circles around the youngest of hard bodies.

It's All about a Decision

What's this story really all about? A bodybuilder? A nutrition and fitness expert? Partially. But the core of Jack Lalanne's saga is about a man who was weak but who made the decision to become strong in body and mind. Lalanne chose to do what was necessary to develop the skills to maintain that strength, stamina, and courage for the rest of his life. When he opened his first health studio in Oakland, California, in 1939, there weren't many takers. As he went door to door to sell his novel idea that a life of vigor and vitality could be discovered through proper diet and exercise, the response was often, "You want me to do what? Go to a gym? Lift weights? Eat better?"

Today he still exercises daily in his private gym, and the last I heard he was still doing pretty well as a confident, always-exploring-opportunities businessman. Not bad for a sickly, ninety-seven pounder from San Francisco who never thought he'd amount to anything. What was the key to his success? Jack Lalanne accepted his past, quit blaming others for his sad state of affairs, decided to get himself out of his sickly state, chose to work his way out of his emotional and physical exhaustion, and made a decision to go to the top. If Jack Lalanne can do it, so can you!

This may be the last chapter of this book, but it's really your exciting, new beginning. How are you doing? Have you been writing in your journal? Have you been reflecting, renewing, and rebuilding? Do you now have a fuller, clearer understand-

---

It's my earnest prayer that you have become filled to overflowing with courage, hope, and excitement for your better future.

---

ing of what may have caused your emotional exhaustion than you did when you started page one? Are you encouraged? Have you become hope filled? It's my earnest prayer that you have become filled to overflowing with courage, hope, and excitement for your better future.

Do you remember back there when you were so totally exhausted that you felt nothing could possibly help you? Do you recall how you once felt so terribly alone, with no visible means of support, feeling no one really cared? Do you remember how you once wanted to run away from it all, when even joining the Foreign Legion sounded like a walk in the park compared to what you were going through? Do you recall how you always used to trouble yourself with a general irritability, mistrust, anger, and even guilt for things you cannot put your finger on now?

Your challenges may not all be in the past, but recovering from emotional exhaustion is a journey more than a destination. It's continuous. Your growth never stops. You just keep getting stronger and stronger. It reminds me of Matthew 7:7, which in the original Greek reads, "Ask, and keep on asking; seek, and keep on seeking; knock, and keep on knocking." I love that verse because it declares the dynamic relationship that God wants us to have with him. He's asking us to embrace a never-say-quit response to life. You will never fully arrive at being strong—because you can always become stronger. Reflect for a moment; ask yourself: Am I further down the road toward inner healing? Has my attitude improved? Have I stopped blaming others for my troubles? If your answer is *yes* to any one of those questions, you are well down the road to regaining control of your life.

Watch Out for Sneak Attacks

While you continue to make progress in becoming resilient in many areas of your life, it's still important that you remember O'Toole's Law. Simply stated, O'Toole's Law says that Murphy *was an optimist.* If something can go wrong with Murphy's Law, it will go ballistic with O'Toole's! With that inescapable truth in mind, let's look at four areas where you'll need to be particularly vigilant in the days ahead to ward off emotional exhaustion and stay strong.

1. *Be alert to ordinary, expected life events.* None of us can escape these. They are the stuff life is made of: high school, trade school, and college graduations, moving across the street or across the world, retiring, getting a promotion, making new friends, or trying to fit into a new neighborhood. Anticipate these events as best you can. If you do not have a plan to accept them in the normal course of living, any one of them could throw you for a loop.

2. *Be alert to the probability of unexpected life events.* These are the shocks and sorrows of life. The death of a spouse or

a child; the tragedy of an automobile accident; getting a call in the middle of the night informing you your best friend has suffered a massive heart attack. These are the really tough times. To be strong is to prepare yourself for these sudden events by building a strong foundational faith in God and in

---

With God-based courage, you can face the ups and downs of life and remain strong. The hard times will not destroy you or drive you into prolonged depression and despair.

---

his ability to see you through. With God-based courage, you can face the ups and downs of life and remain strong. The hard times will not destroy you or drive you into prolonged depression and despair.

3. *Be alert to ongoing events that can drive you crazy.* These can be the everyday emotional killers—like the dog next door that yaps endlessly, the ongoing skirmishes with a spouse, the quarrels with our kids. You may be caring for an aged parent who lingers on in poor health, sapping you financially and emotionally. It could be the sheer boredom with a career that's going nowhere, pressures at work, or unresolved issues with an ex-spouse.

Events such as these tend to have a cumulative effect; if we do not recognize them and deal with them as emotionally healthy persons, they won't be easily resolved. As they weigh us down, we may feel as if we've been ground down to almost nothing. Yet to accept the unacceptable with courage and good humor is one of the ways you can regain control of your life. In God's strength you can be strong in even these most difficult daily situations.

4. *Be alert to stress born of your own personality traits.* I hate to break it to you, but much of your stress is actually related to how you are wired. If you're a perfectionist, life is going to be stressful. In fact it may border on paralysis, with that feeling

that you're never quite up to par and continually comparing yourself to others. If you feel insecure, lack self-worth, and have an overwhelming sense that people are out to get you, you will often allow stress to get the better of you, and it invariably will steer you toward emotional exhaustion.

When, however, you learn to roll with the punches, laugh at our world, and not take yourself too seriously, then what are stressors to others will become little more than annoyances to you. Can you make huge changes in your personality? Probably not. That's why your best solution is to know yourself, be aware of your challenges, and let life be your wise teacher as you anticipate future events.

Improving Your Self-Esteem

As you put all this together in the days ahead, your enhanced self-esteem will be the key to your better future. That's why your prayer should be to ask God to open your eyes to take in his presence more fully. As you accept the truth that comes from the lessons of your experience, you will become increasingly tolerant of your incompleteness. Pray for the courage to face your adversities, and use your life experiences as stepping-stones to the next experience. Doubts, discouragements, and even occasional despair will come your way, but do not indulge them.

Notice, however, that there is a difference between self-esteem and self-worth. Self-worth can come about by having a deep sense of accomplishment for something you've done. It may come from developing a new skill, learning to use a computer, winning the company softball game, or receiving the employee-of-the-month award. Self-esteem, on the other hand, is accepting who you are at your very core. Recognize that you are okay—period! Flawed? Yes. But okay? Absolutely.

As I've read the Scriptures throughout the years, I've come to understand God is telling us that we're not all good, but neither are we all bad. After all, we are created in his image. We are his children, and he is our loving Father. Our assignment is simply to believe God when he says he sees us as

---

As I've read the Scriptures throughout the years, I've come to understand God is telling us that we're not all good, but neither are we all bad.

---

whole persons. We don't need to clean up our mess before he'll love us. It's already okay.

As you work to improve your self-esteem, here are some ways to help you move in the right direction:

1. *Be aware of your self-talk.* When you do something you don't like, start saying something like, "Hey, that's not like me," rather than, "Okay, stupid, you did it again." Feed your mind with decent thoughts about yourself. Don't put yourself down. You don't deserve to be treated that way. Instead of criticizing yourself, learn to forgive yourself. We all have many voices inside speaking to us. Listen only to those that have your best interests at heart.

2. *Speak up for you!* At some point you'll need to work at getting over the fear of expressing yourself. You may want to do this by enrolling in a Dale Carnegie course, joining Toastmasters, or teaching a Bible school class for children. You really do have something important to say, because you are someone of great personal worth. People cannot make you feel lousy about yourself unless you let them, so don't let them. Practice this new strength in small matters and then grow into dealing with the heavier issues. You will become stronger and stronger the more you speak your mind.

You are the executive director of your life. We've already established that God has given you everything you are. Now it's up to you to make the next critical moves. Think for yourself; have the courage to live. Stop letting other people, present circumstances, or ghosts from the past dictate your life. Take the responsibility for your own decisions and bravely move ahead knowing that you were specially designed by God.

3. *Recognize your common characteristics with others.* Yes, you are unique but you also have a great deal in common with all other human beings. The delightful Wizard of Oz, as you may recall, was nothing but a timid, nervous little guy shouting his lungs out through a megaphone. He was not braver than the Lion, more intelligent than the Scarecrow, or more endearing than the Tin Man. He was just like they were, and his alleged wizardry was nothing but smoke and mirrors. Part of feeling good about yourself is to realize that yes, you're unique but at the same time you're not all that different. We're in this thing called the struggle of life together.

4. *Be proud of who you are and what you are becoming.* Optimism about yourself as one designed by a loving heavenly Father enables you to hold your head high, claim a brighter future for yourself, and never give in to negative forces. Thomas Jefferson said, "Resistance to tyrants is obedience to God." One of those tyrants is low self-esteem and a sense of unworthiness. Obey God by being proud of how he lovingly created you and continues to help you grow. It's just as easy—and lots more fun—to look up rather than look down.

Just an Idea

Years ago I saw an illustration that was titled, "It Was Just an Idea." Beneath the title were nine squares with a picture of a light bulb in each square and a quote above each light bulb.

The first light bulb was brightly glowing and said, "I have an idea." The second bulb had lost a little of its glow, saying, "A word of caution." The third bulb was getting dim: "A little too radical." The fourth bulb continues to dim: "I like it myself,

---

I plead with you not to dim the light of the
truth that you have immense worth.

---

but." The fifth bulb is darker yet: "We tried something just like that once." The light is almost gone from the sixth bulb: "Let me play devil's advocate." The light in the seventh bulb is now so faint you can hardly see it: "It's just not us." There is only a slight trace of the eighth bulb: "I wish it were that easy." In the ninth and last square, the bulb is gone for good, and the final quote reads, "Oh, it was just an idea." At the bottom of the page was the caption: "An idea is a fragile thing. Turning it off is much easier than keeping it lit."

I plead with you not to dim the light of the truth that you have immense worth. If you are to recover from emotional exhaustion, you must keep your bulb lit and never let it go out or allow others to put it out. If this is still a challenge for you, I invite you to take this short inventory to help you see—and self-correct—any areas that may still need attention.

1. Do you sometimes catch yourself exaggerating the importance of your job or role?
   almost always   often   rarely   never

2. Do you find yourself checking out your behavior and comparing it to the standards of others?
   almost always   often   rarely   never

3. Are you jealous of the positions, possessions, or opportunities of others?
   almost always   often   rarely   never

4. Is it hard for you to admit that you make mistakes?
   almost always   often   rarely   never

5. Do you neglect your own needs and spend most of your time attending to the needs of others?
   almost always   often   rarely   never

6. Do you put people down so you can feel good about yourself?
   almost always   often   rarely   never

7. Are you a possessive person—unwilling to give others their place or their space?
   almost always   often   rarely   never

8. Are you a bully, demanding your own way?
   almost always   often   rarely   never

9. When a new opportunity or challenge comes your way, does it scare you and make you feel insecure or inadequate?
   almost always   often   rarely   never

10. Is it hard for you to accept compliments and to say a simple "thank you"?
    almost always   often   rarely   never

Almost always or *often* answers to any of these questions indicate you are very much human and, like all of us, need to admit you have some self-esteem issues that need attention. This may be an indication that you need to read this book again and again as well as seek out other sources of help. One helpful book on this subject is by Dr. Frank Freed, *Breaking Free When You're Feeling Trapped* (Harold Shaw).

Getting It All Together

How are you doing? Are you making progress? Are you less hard on yourself? Are you willing to let go, be human, and no longer be paralyzed by perfectionism? With the awareness of each new day and each new life experience, you are collecting the kind of personal data that will help guide you to regaining control of your life. With that in mind, here are seven ways to get it all together.

1. *Protect your self-identity.* Protect who you are without letting negative forces wear you down. When you build yourself up as a worthy person, created and nourished by your loving heavenly Father, you prepare yourself to go the distance. You learn to care for yourself when it's easier not to.

2. *Connect with others.* Don't go it alone! Quality relationships will reduce your emotional exhaustion. At times it may not be easy to connect with family members, but don't give up (unless there is the threat of further abuse). See yourself as a bridge builder, and do your best to develop a network of compassion and relationships that will be there for the long run.

3. *Respect yourself.* When you respect yourself, you are saying *I have value.* Respect means you take responsibility for yourself. Respect promises renewal and keeps you resilient and alive. Respect is your great leap to freedom. When the storms of life try to capsize your boat, respect for yourself will keep you afloat. When you respect yourself, you will not set yourself up to be hurt by others. You will no longer take to heart anyone else's slights or criticisms. Instead, you will disregard the disrespectful things said by others, knowing they need have no effect on you at all.

4. *Make life-giving decisions day after day.* These decisions make your life more meaningful. Affirming, freeing, positive

decisions are the central theme of a healthy, forward-moving life. At The Center when people begin to make significant strides in moving away from emotional exhaustion, this is

---

Respect means you take responsibility for yourself. Respect promises renewal and keeps you resilient and alive. Respect is your great leap to freedom.

---

where they make their greatest progress. Making life-giving decisions helps them navigate through their pain just as the captain of a ship uses his skills to move through the storms, wind, and sandbars at sea— by making one small decision after another, day after day, hour after hour.

5. *Be authentic.* Authentic individuals are really the only ones people can truly relate to. When you're authentic, you are real, no disguises, no games. What people see is what they get. Anything else is a game of defense. The more authentic you are, the more you will be able to truly relate to others and the more empathy you will have for people in pain.

Here's where your past emotional exhaustion can serve as a comfort to those around you, because you've been there. You've suffered the pain of unresolved stress in the past but you've also tunneled through to emotional health. Just as a divorced person can touch the life of another who is going through the trauma of separation or divorce, so you, as the authentic, real article, will be able to touch the heart of the one who's still struggling to survive emotional exhaustion. These past experiences can be among the most powerful tools of all to help keep you strong, resilient, and free from relapsing into old, ineffective behaviors.

6. *Is it laughter you're after?* I hope so, because a good belly laugh every day is one of the greatest tonics for emotional exhaustion. The most wasted day of your life is the one when

you haven't laughed. Consider laughter as "internal jogging." Laugh a lot today, and when you're older, all your wrinkles will be in the right places. Do something today and every day to brighten the life of another.

Laughter is a tranquilizer with no side effects. Make a vow to yourself that you're going to learn to laugh again and laugh often. Don't live as if you were weaned on a pickle. Buy

---

Make a vow to yourself that you're going to learn to laugh again and laugh often. Don't live as if you were weaned on a pickle.

---

some joke books. Rent a few sidesplitting videos. Search for the humor and irony in your life. It's everywhere! Reframe things—see your experience in a different light.

You may recall the story of the man who went to confession. He said to the priest, "Father, I have sinned grievously." "And what have you done that is so bad, my son?" asked the priest. "Oh, Father, I've worked at a lumber yard for twenty years and during that time I have taken a two-by-four home with me every night." "Oh yes, a troubling sin indeed," said the priest. "But I can tell you, my son, there is a solution." "Oh, thank God," said the worker. "What is it?" "Well," said the priest, "can you make a novena?" Said the confessor, "I'm not sure. But if you've got the plans, I've got the lumber!"

7. *Determine to live your life with balance.* Balance will keep you from rigidity. You won't get a hardening of the attitudes. You'll relax more. You'll take the time to smell more daisies. You'll travel lighter. You'll put aside your cases of antacid tablets and you'll start living your life as it was meant to be lived—with joy, with excitement, and to the glory of God. You'll ask for more forgiveness than permission. You'll see yourself as a growing person, willing to take more risks, and

you'll feel the spurts of new growth as you become strong again.

I want to tell you about a little girl named Wilma Rudolph. Wilma was born to an extremely poor family that lived in a small shack in the hills of Tennessee. She was a premature baby, born at four and a half months. She was weak and frail, and no one in her family expected her to live very long. When she was four years old, Wilma had double pneumonia and scarlet fever—a debilitating combination that left her with a paralyzed and useless left leg. Eventually, she had to be fitted with an iron brace. She moved slowly in body, but there was nothing tardy about her spirit—largely because she had a mother who believed in her.

Wilma's mother told her little daughter that despite the clumsy brace, useless leg, and everything the doctors said would happen to her, she could do whatever she wanted to

---

Wilma's mother told her little daughter that despite the clumsy brace, useless leg, and everything the doctors said would happen to her, she could do whatever she wanted to do with her life.

---

do with her life. All she'd ever need to do would be to have faith, persistence, courage, and a never-say-die spirit.

At nine years of age, Wilma did away with the brace. To the astonishment of the doctors and members of her family, she took a step that no one—except her mother—thought she would ever take. In four years' time, she had developed a rhythmic stride that puzzled the doctors even more. Then Wilma got the incredible notion that she would like to be the world's greatest woman runner. Now it was really getting absurd. Run? Run a race? On a leg like that? *Wilma, you're lucky just to be walking!*

So in high school at age thirteen, Wilma decided to enter a race. She came in last—way, way last. In fact Wilma entered every race the school put on, and in every single race she came in last. Her family and friends begged her to quit it—to stop embarrassing herself. But embarrassment was not a factor in Wilma's running. She had a dream. Then one day Wilma Rudolph came in next to last. And then there came a day when she won a race. And from then on, she won every race she ran.

After graduating from high school, Wilma entered Tennessee State University, where she met a coach named Ed Temple. Ed saw the unbelievable courage and spirit of this young woman. He saw a person who believed in herself, and he also saw great, raw, natural talent. He trained Wilma so well—and she was so responsive to his coaching—that the young athlete was given a trip to the Olympic Games.

In the Olympics Wilma was pitted against the greatest woman runner of those times—a German girl named Jutta Heine. Nobody had ever beaten Jutta Heine. But in the one-hundred-meter race, Wilma Rudolph beat her. *Gold medal number one.* She beat her again in the two-hundred-meter race. *Gold medal number two.* Then came the four-hundred-meter relay. It would be Wilma against Jutta in the final leg of the relay. The first two runners on Wilma's team handed the baton over perfectly. But when the third runner handed the baton to Wilma, in her excitement Wilma dropped it, and Wilma saw Jutta speed down the track. It seemed obvious to the crowd that it would be impossible for anyone to catch this fleet and nimble woman. But Wilma did! And now she had *three gold medals.*

How did Wilma do it? She made a decision to be strong despite seemingly insurmountable obstacles. She bumped into life's stumbling blocks and turned them into stepping-stones. It can be the same for you as you master the art of emotionally healthy living.

So now my last questions to you: What do you want to become? What are your greatest dreams? Where do you want your life to take you? Are you ready to put into practice what you've learned in these pages to help you find inner healing and say farewell to emotional exhaustion? I think you are. In fact I know you are. And whenever you think it's too tough and that life's putting too much on your plate, let your mind wander back to Wilma Rudolph, and remember that sometimes you, too, must risk going too far to find out how far you can really go.

Reflect, Renew, Rebuild

Reflect. The following was written by an unknown monk. After reading his thoughts, write your response in your journal. "If I had my life to live over I would relax. . . . I would take fewer things seriously. I would take more chances. I would climb more mountains and swim more rivers. . . . I'd start barefoot earlier in the spring and stay that way later in the fall. I would go to more dances. I would ride more merry-go-rounds. I would pick more daisies."

Renew. In your journal state four reasons why you feel you can stay emotionally strong in this stress-filled world.

Rebuild. I invite you to write the last words in this book. At the back of the book or in your journal, write your action plan for the next sixty days. What will you strive to do to stay strong? How can you keep from relapsing into old, ineffective behaviors? What principles have you learned in this book that will help you say farewell to emotional exhaustion? When you have written your comments, I invite you to share them with me. They will be held in strictest confidence. All the best, and God bless you, my friend.

Appendix

Suggested Healthy Eating

Category	Foods to Focus On	Foods to Minimize
Beverages	Herbal teas, fresh fruit and vegetable juices, spring water	Alcohol, cocoa, coffee, canned, pasteurized, or processed juices
dairy products	Milk, butter, cottage cheese, split milk, fermented milk products (yogurt, kefir, buttermilk), ghee	Processed and imitation butter, ice cream, or creamers; excessive hard cheese
fruit	Any fresh, frozen, stewed, or dried	Fruit canned in sugar syrup
grains	Whole grains and whole grain products—cereals, breads, muffins, chapatis (rye, oat, wheat, bran, buckwheat, millet), unpolished white rice (Basmati), whole seeds (sesame, pumpkin, sunflower)	White flour products, polished rice, highly processed grains
nuts	All fresh nuts and nut butters Almonds—raw without skin, roasted with skin	Salted nuts, oil roasted nuts

Category	Foods to Focus On	Foods to Minimize
oils	Cold-processed oils, Saturated oils (olive oil and peanut oil)	Shortening, refined fats and oils, excessively heated oils, hydrogenated fats and oils
seasonings	Herbs, garlic, onion, ginger, parsley, cayenne, pepper, green and red chiles	Salt, artificial seasonings
soups	Any fresh	Highly processed commercial
sprouts	All—wheat, lentil, alfalfa, mung	None
sweets	Raw honey, unsulfured molasses, carob, malt, maple syrup	Refined sugars (white, brown, turbinado), chocolate, candy, commercial syrups
vegetables	All raw, steamed, baked, or fresh potatoes, beets, greens, cabbage	Canned, highly processed, overly cooked

ADDITIONAL INFORMATION: Avoid smoke, exhausts, sprayed foods, additives, preservatives, MSG, artificial colors and flavors. If eating meat, minimize quantity and consume leanest portions. Obtain from least contaminated source possible. Drink a minimum of 1 liter fresh water daily in addition to other liquids.

Vitamins and Health

Vitamin	Dosage	Depleting Factors	Augmenting Nutrients
B-1 Thiamine	10–500 mg	Alcohol, antibiotics, birth control pills, coffee, diuretics, diarrhea, excess sugar, fever, raw clams and oysters, stress, and surgery.	Vitamin B-complex, B-2, C, D, folic acid, manganese, niacin, sulphur, zinc. B-1 intake should equal B-2 intake.
B-2 Riboflavin	10-100 mg	Alcohol, birth control pills, coffee, excessive surgar, tobacco Need increases in proportion to muscular work.	Vitamin B-complex, B-1, C, niacin, phosphorus, zinc.
B-3 Niacin	50–5,000 mg	Alcohol, antibiotics, birth control pills, coffee, corn, excessive sugar and starches, growth periods, illness, physical labor, tissue trauma.	Vitamin B-complex, B-1, B-2, C, phosphorus, zinc.
B-5 Panothenic acid	2,500 mg	Alcohol, coffee, insecticides, sleeping pills, stress.	Vitamin B-complex, B-6, B-12, folic acid, C, zinc.
B-6 Pyridoxine	10–500 mg	Aging, alcohol, birth control pills, heart attack, insecticides, radiation exposure, sleeping pills, tobacco.	Vitamin B-complex, B-1, B-2, C, linolenic acid, magnesium, potassium, sodium, zinc.
B-12 Cyanocobalamin	50–5,000 mg	Aging, alcohol, coffee, insecticides, iron, calcium and B-2 deficiency, laxatives, sleeping pills, tobacco.	Vitamin B-complex, B-6, folic acid, inositol, C, calcium, potassium, sodium, zinc.
B-15 Panagamic acid	50–600 mg	Alcohol, birth control pills, coffee, insecticides, sleeping pills.	Vitamin B-complex, C, E, zinc.
Choline	50–2,500 mg	Alcohol, birth control pills, coffee, excessive sugar, insecticides, sleeping pills.	Vitamin A, B-complex, B-12, folic acid, inositol, linolenic acid, zinc.

Biological Function	Deficiency Symptoms	Conditions Treated
Affects absorption, digestion, appetite, blood building, and carbohydrate metabolism; corrects and prevents beriberi; enhances learning ability; promotes growth, resistance to infection, and proper nerve function.	Beriberi, fatigue, intestinal disorders, irritability, nerve degeneration, numbness of hands and feet, poor lacitation and appetite, shortness of breath, slow heart beat, ulcers, weakness.	Alcoholism, anemia, beriberi, constipation, diabetes, diarrhea, headaches, heart failure, indigestion, leg cramps, mental illness, nausea, shingles, stress.
Affects antibody and red blood cell formation; aids iron assimilation and protein metabolism; helps skin, digestive tract, and eyes stay healthy.	Cataracts, digestive disturbances, hair loss, impaired lactation, lack of stamina, pellagra, reduced tissue respiration, retarded growth.	Acne, alcoholism, arthritis, baldness, cataracts, diabetes, diarrhea, digestion, multiple sclerosis, pellagra, stress, ulcers, vaginitis.
Affects circulation; promotes hormone production, growth, hydrochloric acid production; helps maintain nervous system, metabolism, and respiration; reduces cholesterol level.	Appetite loss, canker sores, depression, fatigue, halitosis, headaches, indigestion, insomnia, muscular weakness, nausea, nerve disorders, skin problems.	Acne, arteriosclerosis, baldness, diabetes, diarrhea, epilepsy, halitosis, high blood pressure, leg cramps, migraine, poor circulation, schizophrenia, stress, tooth decay.
Affects antibody formation, carbohytrate metabolism, stimulates growth; helps maintain healthy skin and nerves; maintains blood sugar level, stimulates adrenals.	Adrenal exhaustion, depression, diarrhea, hair loss, hypoglycemia, intestinal disorders, kidney problems, nerve disorders, premature aging, skin disorders.	Acne, allergies, arthritis, baldness, cystitis, digestive disorders, epilepsy, fatigue, fracture, hypoglycemia, leg cramps, mental illness, tooth decay.
Affects antibody formation; controls levels of magnesium in blood and tissue; aids digestion; maintains sodium/potassium balance and cholesterol levels; aids metabolism of fats.	Acne, anemia, arthritis, behavioral changes, convulsion in infants, dizziness, hair loss, irritability, learning disabilities, swelling, weakness.	Alcoholism, anemia, arteriosclerosis, baldness, cystitis, high blood cholesterol, mental illness, morning sickness, muscular and nervous disorders, stress.
Affects appetite, blood cell formation, cell longevity; stimulates normal metabolism of nerve tissue; aids in protein, fat, and carbohydrate metabolism and utilization of iron.	Menstrual disturbances, nerv-ousness, soreness and weakness in extremities, symptoms of schizophrenia, and walking and talking difficulties.	Alcoholism, allergies, asthma, arteriosclerosis, bursitis, epilepsy, fatigue, hypoglycemia, insomnia, overweight, peptic ulcer, pernicious anemia, tuberculosis.
Affects cell oxidation, respiration, glandular system, and nervous system; stimulates glucose and fat protein metabolism.	Diminished oxidation of cells, glandular and nervous disorders, heart disease.	Alcoholism, arteriosclerosis, cancer, emphysema, fever, high colesterol, hypertension, hypoxia, poor circulation, premature aging, rheumatic fever, rheumatism.
Affects health of liver, kdney, and nerve tissue and utilization of fats; prevents gallstones; with inositol is basic constituent of lecithin.	Bleeding ulcers, fatty deposits in liver, growth problems, heart trouble, high blood pressure, kidney blockage.	Alcoholism, asthma, arteriosclerosis, constipation, dizziness, hair problems, headaches, heart problems, hepatitis, high blood cholesterol, hypoglycemia, insomnia.

Notes

Chapter 1: Coming Apart at the Seams

1. *Newsweek,* 6 March 1995.

Chapter 2: The Long Journey from Darkness to Light

1. Paul Johnson, *Modern Times: The World from the Twenties to the Eighties* (Harper and Row, 1983).

2. See Gregory L. Jantz, *Healing the Scars of Emotional Abuse* (Grand Rapids: Revell, 1995).

Chapter 3: The Poisons of Anger, Fear, and Guilt

1. David Augsburger, *The Freedom of Forgiveness* (Chicago: Moody Press, 1970), 63.

2. Carol Kent, "Taming Your Fears: Where to Go When Life Gets Scary," *Servant* 40 (fall 1995): 4–6.

Chapter 4: Forgiveness

1. Charles R. Swindoll, *Killing Giants, Pulling Thorns* (Grand Rapids: Zondervan, 1993), 50.

2. Herbert J. Freudenberger, "Today's Troubled Men," *Psychology Today* (December 1987), 46–47.

3. Ibid.

Chapter 5: Removing the Ghosts from Your Past

1. Helen Keller, *The Story of My Life* (Garden City, N.Y.: Doubleday, 1954).

Chapter 6: Self-Care

1. Gregory L. Jantz, *Losing Weight Permanently: Secrets of the 2% Who Succeed* (Wheaton, Ill.: Harold Shaw, 1996).

2. Covert Bailey, *The New Fit or Fat* (Boston: Houghton Mifflin, 1991), 84.

3. John Robert McFarland, *Now That I Have Cancer, I Am Whole: Meditations for Cancer Patients and Those Who Love Them* (Kansas City, Mo.: Andrews and McMeel, 1993).

4. Jantz, *Losing Weight,* 110.

5. Ibid.

6. Charlie Jones, *Humor Is Tremendous* (Wheaton, Ill.: Tyndale, 1988).

7. Eugene Peterson, *The Message* (Colorado Springs: NavPress, 1995).

Chapter 7: Six Disciplines for Eliminating Self-Defeating Attitudes

1. Robert Eliot, *From Stress to Strength: How to Lighten Your Load and Save Your Life* (New York: Bantam, 1995).

Chapter 8: The Joy of Confident Living

1. Denis Waitley, *Empires of the Mind* (New York: William and Morrow, 1995), 210. Used by permission.

Chapter 9: Living Right-Side Up in an Upside-Down World

1. See Jantz, *Healing the Scars of Emotional Abuse.*

Dr. Gregory L. Jantz is a bestselling author, consultant, and keynote speaker. Dr. Jantz holds a PhD in counseling psychology and is the founder and executive director of The Center for Counseling and Health Resources, Inc., a mental health and chemical dependency treatment agency. Over the past fifteen years Dr. Jantz has developed and implemented "whole person" care programs for individuals and businesses.

Dr. Jantz hosts a daily call-in radio show in the Seattle area. The author of six books, he is a popular and frequent guest on radio and television talk shows across the nation.

You may contact the author at

The Center
P.O. Box 700
Edmonds, WA 98020
425-771-5166
fax: 425-670-2807
email: drjantz@aol.com
toll free seminar and information line: 1-888-771-5166

Visit his website: www.aplaceofhope.com